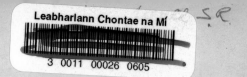
Joyce Grenfell was born in London in 1910. She made her first stage appearance in 1939 using her own material and went on to tour the world with solo performances. In addition she made countless film and television appearances and wrote two volumes of autobiography.

For her songs her main collaborator was Richard Addinsell who set more than fifty of her lyrics to music and who is widely known as the composer of *The Warsaw Concerto*. She also wrote songs with Donald Swann and with William Blezard who was her accompanist for many years.

Joyce Grenfell died in 1979.

Also by Joyce Grenfell

JOYCE GRENFELL

Turn Back the Clock
her best monologues and songs

Futura

A Futura Book

Copyright © Joyce Grenfell 1977, 1978
Joyce Grenfell Memorial Trust 1983

First published in Great Britain in 1983
by Macmillan London Limited
London and Basingstoke

This edition published in 1984
by Futura Publications, a Division of
Macdonald & Co (Publishers) Ltd
London & Sydney
Reprinted 1984, 1988

ISBN 0 7088 2602 4

Printed and bound in Great Britain by
Collins, Glasgow

Futura Publications
A Division of
Macdonald & Co (Publishers) Ltd
66–73 Shoe Lane
London EC4P 4AB

A member of Maxwell Pergamon Publishing Corporation plc

To all Joyce's known and unknown friends

Contents

Chronology

(including principal stage appearances)

1910	Born 10 February
1936/9	Radio critic for *The Observer*
1939/40	*Farjeon's Little Revue*
1940/1	*Farjeon's Diversion*
1942	*Farjeon's Light and Shade*
1944/5	Entertained troops
1945/6	*Sigh No More* by Noël Coward
1947/8	*Tuppence Coloured*
1951/2	*Penny Plain*
1954	*Joyce Grenfell Requests the Pleasure* London
1955	*Joyce Grenfell Requests the Pleasure* New York
1956/60	Concert tours with solo shows to many countries including USA, Canada and Australia
1962	*Seven Good Reasons* London. UK concert tour

1963	Solo show London at Theatre Royal, Haymarket
1966	Solo show London at Queen's Theatre
1971/5	BBC television programme *Face the Music*
1976	Published autobiography *Joyce Grenfell Requests the Pleasure*
1977	Published *George, Don't Do That*
1977	Published *Stately as a Galleon*
1979	Published autobiography *In Pleasant Places*

many films from 1949 included:
Stage Fright, The Happiest Days of your Life, Laughter in Paradise, Genevieve, The Million Pound Note, The Belles of St Trinians (plus others in the same series), *The Americanization of Emily, The Yellow Rolls-Royce.*

numerous radio and television appearances plus further concert tours.
contributions to various magazines.

| 1979 | Died 30 November |

Biographies

RICHARD ADDINSELL was born in 1904 and died
in 1977. He began his career as a composer after
leaving Oxford in 1925. He collaborated with
Clemence Dane on a number of productions including
*Adam's Opera, Come of Age, L'Aiglon, The Happy
Hypocrite* and *Alice in Wonderland.* Plays for which
he wrote incidental music include Emlyn Williams'
Trespass and Jean Anouilh's *Ring Around the Moon.*
He also composed the scores for many major films
including *Goodbye Mr Chips, The Prince and the
Showgirl, The Greengage Summer, Blithe Spirit, The
Roman Spring of Mrs Stone* and *Dangerous
Moonlight,* which included his most celebrated work
The Warsaw Concerto. He began his thirty-year
collaboration with Joyce Grenfell in 1941, composing
the majority of the music to her own lyrics.

WILLIAM BLEZARD has been musical director for many West End productions and worked with Marlene Dietrich, Max Wall and, most notably, Joyce Grenfell with whom he wrote many songs. He also gives recitals, works regularly on television and has composed many chamber and orchestral works.

DONALD SWANN'S name will always be associated with that of the late Michael Flanders. Together they wrote and performed such shows as *At the Drop of a Hat* and *At the Drop of Another Hat* which took them from the West End to Broadway. More recently he has divided his time between composing and performing. His one-man show *An Evening with Donald Swann* has taken him all over the world.

I
REVUE PIECES

Useful and Acceptable Gifts

At dinner with the Nicholses and Potters I found myself describing a talk our Women's Institute had heard at the monthly meeting in the Recreation Hall at Cliveden a few days earlier. The visiting speaker told us about Useful and Acceptable Gifts and how to make something from nothing. She had an unlocalised accent of great daintiness and spoke carefully, every consonant sharply finished and smartly delivered with all her vowels aslant. Her lecture was a collector's item and I collected it. It wasn't only what she said that was worth garnering but also the way she said it. My audience was responsive and I made the most of being the centre of attention. We sat on at the candle-lit table while I got 'possessed' as I used to do in the dormitory at boarding-school. There was no need to invent any of it. The stuff was rich grist and I simply milled it. Considering what a lot I got out

17

of that talk I suppose I should have discovered the lecturer's name and sent her a royalty, but at the time I didn't know about such things.

Madam President, Fellow Institute Members, good evening. This evening I am going to tell you a little bit about my useful and acceptable gifts, and these gifts are not only easy to make but ever so easy to dispose of. I see several of you ladies have your eye on the boutonnière in my lapel — it *is* pretty, isn't it? — and I am going to tell you how to make one just like it. First of all you must obtain some empty beech-nut husk clusters. These are to be found beneath beech trees almost any time after about the middle of September onwards. Cleanse your husks thoroughly. And then wire them on to stalks or stems. (You will find six or eight are ample for a boutonnière.) Now, before you *colour* you must decide what flower it is you are making. Mine are wood anemonies — shell-pink without, and a deeper rose within. (Sometimes I like to use just a *suspicion* of gold or silver! I like to feel that we take Nature's gifts and make them even lovelier.) Now, when you are making beech-nut husk flowers do not confine yourself to boutonnières. Be *bold* about it! You can make great sprays of lupes, or delphs.

(If anybody wants to take notes I shan't mind a bit.)

Well, next we come to a more serious gift — waste-paper baskets, or should I say more accurately — waste-paper basket tins, for they are made from manufacturers' biscuit tins, and in order to obtain these you must make love to your grocer and wheedle him into giving one to you. First, cleanse your tin

18

thoroughly and then remove all existing advertising matter. In order to obtain my unusual mosaic design you are going to want some pieces of wallpaper patterns. (I prefer beige tones myself.) Tear your paper up into scraps — the smaller the better — and then paste the pieces all over the *outside* of the tin — higgledy-piggledy, in what you might call a crazy-paving design; and when the pieces are quite firm, outline them in black Indian ink, and you will find you have not only a useful waste-paper basket, but a very unusual piece of modernistic furniture as well.

So much for tins. And lastly we come to what I like to call my comic turn! Dicky Calendars — Dicky Calendars. Dicky is made from two india-rubbers, or, as we called them when I went to school, bunjies! You will want a small one for the head and a strong sturdy one for the body. The head must be joined *to* the body, so obtain some strong wire and pass it through the head and right through poor Dicky's body to emerge as his legs. Mount him on a cardboard paper stand, give him two bright pin eyes and a pheasant or chicken's feather for a tail, and then, with a calendar on a jaunty ribbon round his neck, Dicky is ready to keep up to date!

Ladies, it is our duty as women to beautify our surroundings. Now when you get home I want you to seek out materials to make yourself Useful and Acceptable Gifts. Good evening.

THE LITTLE REVUE, 1939

Different Kinds of Mothers

All the mothers are in their middle thirties.
The American comes from the Mid-West; the
Understanding Mother is from the Chelsea—
Kensington border; and the second of the
three is a native of Bucks, where words like
'a little girl' become 'a littoo gurw'. The face
I used for this character came as a result
of wondering, as I looked at myself in a
looking-glass, what would happen, not only
to my face but also to my speech, if I put
my tongue in front of my lower teeth and
spoke. (Try it and see.) That's the face and
the sound I used later for another Bucks
villager in 'A Terrible Worrier'.

An American Mother

Now, Muriel dear, Mother doesn't want to see that
face. We're going to learn this little pome for Grandma's
birthday, and I don't want to hear any more nonsense.
I want you to start right from the beginning, after
Mother; that is the way to learn. 'Hail to thee, blithe
spirit, Bird thou never wert'.

Come on, Muriel, dear, 'Hail . . . Hail to thee blithe
spirit'.

What does blithe mean? Blithe means happy spirit
— spirit full of joy and happiness. 'Hail to thee, *blithe*

20

spirit, Bird though never wert'.

I don't know what it was, dear, if it wert not a bird. No, it is not a silly pome, Muriel; it's a very beautiful pome. And Muriel, we don't learn poitry only because it is beautiful but because it teaches us to speak beautifully. You're going to find that very useful later on in life.

It is called 'To a Skylark' by Percy Bysshe Shelley. Bysshe doesn't mean a thing, dear, it's his name. His mother was probably a Miss Bysshe.

Come on, dear, we aren't getting any place at all; and Muriel, stick in your stomach. Now let's start right from the beginning, after Mother. 'To a Skylark' — Yes — by Percy — go on — Bysshe — Muriel! Where did you learn that word?

You go right upstairs and wash out your mouth at once!

A Village Mother

Ernie, you thank Mrs Tucker for giving you that beautiful lollipop. Oh, he's better now, Mrs Tucker, but he did give us a turn last week. Tuesday it was, about dinner-time. He come in from school, got his head all on the one side. I said to his Dad, don't you think Ernie is a funny colour? His Dad said he did. That was Tuesday. Wednesday he was still like this. I couldn't make it out. We was having a lovely piece of knuckle for dinner, but he couldn't touch it. Just sips of tea, sips of tea. I said to his Dad, 'Look, if he's no better by tomorrow morning you've got to get your bike out and go get the doctor to him.' But it was raining on Thursday. Friday, he was still like this. I tucked him up in bed and give him a hot-water bottle between his neck and his shoulder; but I couldn't get him a bit comfy. I was just going down the garden to get my bike out to go get the doctor to him when he gives a yell — 'Mum,' he says, 'Mum!' I go upstairs; he's been having a choke. Cough, cough, cough. I thought he was going. All at once up comes a conker! Been lodged in his neck all that time. Oh, he was relieved. Wasn't you, duckie. And do you know why? Because it was a conker he'd borrowed.

The Understanding and Rather English Mother

Harriet — Harriet, darling — in bed already? Good, because I want to talk to you, darling. I want to talk to you very frankly. Now, I'm not an interfering mother, and I hope I never shall be. This is your life, and you've got to do what you want with it. All Daddy and I want is your happiness. That's all we want. You see, darling, growing up — well, being grown-up, then — is a very trying time. Don't think I don't know because I do. I know exactly. So does Daddy. We both know exactly. Harriet, I'm afraid you think the reason we don't like Leon is because Leon is a conjurer. Darling, that's not the point at all. It's marvellous to be a conjurer. Daddy says he can't think how he does it. But have you considered what it would be like to be a conjurer's wife? Do you think you could stand it? I know I couldn't. Rabbits popping in and out of things all the time. And it seems to me *that* is your problem. Do you think you could be really happy married to a middle-aged Portuguese conjurer? No, darling, we won't discuss it any more tonight because I want you to sleep well and look pretty tomorrow morning. And darling, I'm not in the least worried about you. Nor is Daddy. There is *nothing* to be worried about. I'm not in the *least* worried.

THE LITTLE REVUE, 1939

Head Girl

... I say, you Juniors, squattez-vous down in front and leave those pews at the back for your elders and betters and QUIET please. Quiet. Well, this isn't an ordinary school meeting. As a matter of fact, I've got some frightfully exciting news for you: Miss Torpor is going to get married ... which of course is frightfully bad luck on us but absolutely marvellous luck for Miss Torpor. No more jolly sing-songs up in the Torp's room, worse luck, still it is good news. He's called Dr Cliffwick, and he's been out in British East Africa for absolutely ages, only he's back in England now and settled in Potter's Bar, and when they are married in the next hols they will live at Potter's Bar which will be absolutely marvellous for them.

Well, the rest of the Sixth and myself thought it would be great fun to give Miss Torpor a present and we've had one or two ideas. But, as this is a *real* school present, absolutely any one of you may make suggestions ... even the measliest juniors in front ... and Alison will be at the door to take down your ideas on your way out, but meanwhile we'll tell you what we've thought. Mavis suggests silver candlesticks for the piano ... if we get enough L.S.D. ... about which I Hae Me Doots. And Dulcie thought one of those gold brooches in the shape of a tennis racket with a pearl for a ball — because Miss Torpor is Games as well as Maths. And someone has suggested doilies for the dining-room table, gram. records, kitchen utensils and a pet. And the *Encyclopaedia Britannica* or whatever it's called, only I think that's a bit too schooly.

And then there's my own idea which I expect you'll think is absolutely feeble: I happened to sit next to Miss Torpor at brekker and I said to her, 'Which bit of the school do you like best? And she said, 'You know the bit behind the lab., by the pond and the pine trees? Well, there.' So I had what I think is rather a brainy wheeze: why shouldn't we get the Sketching Club to get up a sketching competish? We could have the entries frightfully impartially judged . . . by the staff or some-one, and then we could get the winning one frightfully nicely mounted and frightfully nicely framed and then it really would be a real school present and remind Miss Torpor always of St E.'s. I expect you think it's a Ghastly Scheme. Oh well, a poor thing but mine own.

And now that I've got you here, I've got to give you a bit of a jaw. I absolutely hate being a wet blanket but a head girl has to be a lot of things she doesn't much like, worse luck. Miss Chuddington isn't a bit pleased with the spirit in the school just now. The other day she happened to go into the Plum Dormitory bath-room and there she came upon two girls washing at the same basin at the same time. Well, that is not the school spirit, is it? So in the future, let's pull our socks up and see if we can't remember: One Girl, One Basin.

Sorry if I've been gloomy after Miss Torpor's glorious news, and now it's jolly nearly time for after-noon school, so will you file out quietly please, and if you brought chairs in with you, carry them out quietly please. QUIETLY PLEASE.

THE LITTLE REVUE, 1939

Canteen in Wartime

Mrs Boller — Mrs Boller — your sausage rolls have come and they are absolutely lovely! Almost as much sausage as roll. Will you count them very carefully before you let them get on to the counter? Angel, bless you.

Oh, she's such a divine woman, and *so* reliable. I mean I really can count on her coming once a week. And the men absolutely worship her — all that lovely grey hair — in fact they'd work her to death if I let them. But you know she really isn't *quite* as young as she might be so I do try and protect her all I can.

Mrs Boller, when you've counted all your lovely sausage rolls, will you be a dear and carry all the glasses from the sink to the counter? Angel, bless you.

Well now, Cissie, how many sandwiches are we making tonight?

My *dear*!

Well, they absolutely wolfed them last night. I saw one lovely Canadian have four. I ask you! I always feel ham is so frightfully leaden, don't you?

Look, will you be most awfully nice and sit next to Cissie and help her with her spreading? Do you know, I'm most frightfully silly and I cannot listen when I'm introduced and I cannot remember what you said your name was. Mrs Tinsley Hatten. Will you please forgive me for *not* knowing your name, and will you be a dear and sit next to Cissie and help her with her spreading, and then, if you would pass it along to me, I pop the ham in and then I pass it along to Sybil and she cuts it up. I'm most frightfully silly but I do feel that if one has a system one does get done in half the time. I'm sure you'll get quite used to it.

Sybil, did you happen to see the state the urns were in again last night? Yes, darling, I know we had an awful rush but all the same if she would only get some kind of method and system I'm sure she could keep those urns lovely and clean and shiny the entire time.

But don't listen to me. I'm an absolute lunatic where cleanliness is concerned. Well, I do think it makes the WHOLE difference.

Yes, Miss Mouser?

OH! How TRAGIC! No doughnuts.

Mrs Boller — NO DOUGHNUTS. Well, what are we going to do?

Well, we must have something sweet. They do so need it, the lambs.

Is the little boy still there?

Well, ask him if he's got any of those flans? (They are so horrid.)

Oh, GOOD. Saved again, Mrs Boller. He HAS got flans.

Miss Mouser, I'm going to ask you the most enormous favour. Would you be a dear and come and sit here and finish my hamming for me while I give out

26

the orders for the day? Angel, bless you.

Well now, is everybody listening?

Sybil, you and Lady Bucket are washers-up as usual.

Cissie, you and Mrs Boller go on the counter for the first half and then change places with Grace and Miss Mouser for the second.

I'm most awfully silly, Mrs Tinsley Hatten, but I'm not allowed to carry things. So I have to be the most awful nuisance and get in everybody's way doing all the little odd jobs. And I can't help with the washing-up either, because I'm not allowed to get wet.

Do you know, I believe it would amuse you enormously to wash up. It's the greatest possible fun. I only wish I was allowed to do it.

Well now, is everybody ready?

Mrs Wink, your urns are lovely and clean and shiny? Good. (She can do it when she tries, you see.)

Mrs Boller, I'm sure the counter looks lovely.

(You know, Mrs Tinsley Hatten, Mrs Wink is a divine woman and I simply couldn't possibly do without her, but she *cannot* keep her urns clean and I always feel the men notice it. *Mais, c'est la guerre!*)

You know, my trouble is I've got too much sense of humour. When trouble comes along I simply laugh it away.

Oh, Miss Mouser! You've finished all my hamming for me. I do feel ashamed. Now, are you all ready? Then be off with you.

Look, I'm just going to slip away if you really think you can manage without me. I am just the least little bit exhausted. . . . Angels . . . Bless you!

DIVERSION, 1940

Local Library

I'm afraid I've got to disappoint you about the new Angela Thirkell again, Miss Taylor. I don't know when to promise it for. They've had it at the Vicarage for over three weeks, and you know what they are — just the one subscription for the whole family. Would you like to try *Pretty Polly*? They say it's quite lively.

Well, look, dear, you have a bit of a browse round while I look after Mrs Cruden. That's right.

And how is Mrs Cruden?

Good. And how did you like it?

Oh, what a shame, I told you it was depressing, didn't I? What a shame. We'll have to find you something a bit more cheerful next time, won't we? What about an Ian Hay? Don't feel funny? Oh, you are in a bad way, aren't you? Just a minute, though — if that London parcel is in I think I'm going to have something you are going to like. Excuse me.

Miss Hervey, is the London parcel in yet? Oh thanks, Miss Hervey.

The posts are shocking.

What about that gipsy novel serialised in the *Chronicle* a week or so ago? Don't like gipsies? Well, what about a Life, then? Doctors' lives are very interesting, aren't they? My sister was telling me about one she was reading in the train on the way to work ... called *Medicine Man Awheel*, it's all about a doctor living at Herne Bay ... goes everywhere by bike. Marvellous, isn't it? No, dear, I'm afraid you can't have it because my sister's got it. Well, what about a hospital book? A hospital book is always nice, isn't it? Let's see what we've got. *Just Pickle My Bones* — that's about a hospital. *Cut it Out* — that's about a hospital. *Ill at Ease* — that's about a nursing home. Look dear, would you like to take those over to the table for a good browse while I take care of this gentleman? That's right . . .

Good morning, it's Mr Pell, isn't it? Oh, Mr Druggit, I'm awfully sorry, but you're awfully like Mr Pell — just the same build and you both wear those knitted gloves. Did you like it? Good. Well, would you like to slip it back into my Classics shelf for me? No, it's the little one, right at the top. No, I haven't read it myself, but I saw the picture. Well, what are you going to have this time? Oh you've got your eye on my Guaranteed shelves — 'A' subscriptions; yours is a 'D'. No non-fiction, no biography, no new works. What a shame. What did you see up there? *Ego* 7. Well, I don't know what you'd call it — it's by a theatrical critic and it's half in French, half in English, and it's about a lot of old-fashioned actresses and a collection of umbrellas the author's made. No, I'm afraid you can't. Not without a transfer. Will you have a bit of a poke round while I finish off Miss Taylor? — I think she's got what she wants.

Hullo, what's Miss Taylor got hold of? *While Both Ends Burn* — don't say I didn't warn you if you find it a trifle outspoken.

No — it isn't that — well, it's just silly, really. Yes, it did have some quite good reviews, I'll admit that. I think it was the *Globe* said it was a 'difficult subject bravely tackled' . . . but I didn't like it. Still, you may, dear. How are the pups?.

Good — and mother?

Bye-bye, dear.

When I look at you properly, Mr Druggit, I don't know how I could have confused you with Mr Pell — oh, he's a dear soul really, but all he wants is travel, travel, travel, and I can't keep him supplied. Comes here and says to me, 'Peter Fleming been anywhere lately?' I tell him there's nowhere to go.

Hullo, you got what you want? More Dickens! Aren't you the glutton for the one pen? I hope you enjoy it . . . excuse me a minute.

Yes, Miss Hervey? Oh good — just in time for the weekend.

Mrs Cruden, Mrs Cruden, can you come in again after lunch? Good — I'm going to have just what you are going to like — a whole batch of new love tales for you to curl up with! See you later, then, bye-bye, dear.

DIVERSION, 1940

There is Nothing New
to Tell You

Music by Richard Addinsell

The stamp is on the envelope,
I've written on your name —
It's very nearly midnight,
But I'm writing just the same.

There is nothing new to tell you,
The days go drifting by,
And I hardly have to tell you,
   just why.

It was raining here this morning,
It rained when first we met —
So I like a rainy morning,
And yet, it won't let me forget.

I'm feeling fine but I wish you were here,
I need you still, I always will,
   my dear.

There is nothing new to tell you,
We've said it all before —
But I thought I'd like to say it, once more
You are all I adore.

I'm Going to See You Today

Music by Richard Addinsell

This is our red-letter-day,
It's come at last you see;
Couldn't really be a better day,
It's meant for you and me.
This day we've been awaiting, patiently.
It is perfection to me, for —

I'm going to see you today,
All's well with my world;
And the people that I meet,
As I hurry down the street,
Seem to know I'm on my way,
Coming to you.
This is a beautiful day,
I'm treading on air,
And my feet have taken to wings,
My heart with happiness sings,
I'll see you today.

The waiting days that dragged along
Were colourless and slow,
Those weary, dreary days that lagged along
As if they'd never go

Are now at last behind us, finally,
All is enchantment to me, for —

I'm going to see you today,
All's well with my world;
And the people that I meet,
As I hurry down the street,
Seem to know I'm on my way,
Coming to you.
This is a beautiful day,
I'm treading on air,
And my feet have taken to wings
My heart with happiness sings
I'll see you today.

Situation Vacant

The scene of my sketch is a domestic agency. Time 1942. A lady is desperately searching for a housekeeper.

I wonder if you'd be most awfully kind and let me put my name down on your waiting list for a working housekeeper? Oh, I know, of *course*, you haven't anyone on your books at all and there isn't the *least* chance of you being able to help me, but I do feel that one has at least taken a step in the right direction if one can only get one's name down somewhere. I can't seem to get anyone to take my name down, and honestly, mine is a frightfully easy job and I'm absolutely sure any housekeeper would simply adore it if only she could *hear* about it. You see, I'm out all day on my war job and my husband is in Scotland, and the children are almost entirely with my mother, and I only have coffee and toast for breakfast and almost nothing for dinner at night, and I don't use hardly any silver because of the war — so there is almost literally NOTHING to do.

It's a country post — but there's a market town only five miles away with a *huge* cinema and wonderful shops, and the buses go simply whizzing down a road that is only a few minutes' run across a couple of fields from us and over a potty little stile — or you could go round by the road but it's rather longer and we only use it in wet weather when the field gets flooded. And there's a Women's Institute in the next village and hundreds of whist drives all over the place in aid of the Red Cross and the Russians and things, and we've got a MIXED choral society and an evacuee mothers' club and a fête every August Bank Holiday — it's frightfully gay, truly it is.

Oh no, it's a TINY house — I mean literally minute. Well, there's our bedroom and my husband's dressing room, and the children's rooms and the spare room and of course the housekeeper's room with its own *bath-sitting room* next door. You hardly see the bath at all because it's so well tucked away under an eave. There's a wireless there and her own sofa and a set of Corinthian Bagatelle if she likes — we had one once who played it all night, so you never know — and there's a sewing machine and an ironing board, just supposing she sort of felt, well, maybe, like doing a little something to my underclothes. And then there's the dining room and the drawing room and the children's nursery-schoolroom and the kitchen. I know it doesn't sound small but it's on a *tiny* scale and really very easy to look after. You know, I don't want any waiting on — all I want is some clean, happy person who can cook just a little and answer the telephone and not get called up. Of course, it makes it nicer if she happens to be honest and sober at the same time, doesn't it?

Look. I feel in all fairness I ought to tell you that a place called the Practical Peasant Agency in Sussex have offered me an unrestricted Croat of sixty-five. But you see she's used to titled people and she doesn't speak any English and she's not allowed to cook after sunset for some religious reason, so you see I thought if I could find someone just a little easier it would be nicer and you see all I want is a little kindness, so won't you please, *please*, let me put my name down on your waiting list waiting to get on to your books?

Oh, thank you so much.

I wonder if I might have a glass of water . . .

LIGHT AND SHADE, 1942

End of Affair

(Coward-type play)

Why must we spoil it all now? It's — it's all meant so
much to me, Bertram. No, my dear, I don't hate you
— why should I? We've shared so much that this — this
hurt is but a gallant banner to tittup in the breezes
of whatever is to come. Am I happy? What, after all,
is happiness? Our life together — not long as men
count time but eternity for me. All the memories —
nostalgic little pictures, my dear — your hay fever in
Rouen — anchovy toast — the absurb little Tyrolean
hats we shared! Oh, my sweet — Sydenham public
baths. No, don't — because it's over, Bertram, over
and done with and we are civilised enough to recognise
the word 'finis' written across the page. What am I
going to do? Be fearless and gay and even a little
foolish perhaps — who knows? I don't hate you. No,
I don't. My dear, I ought to know. I went into this
thing with my eyes open and I am not a child — not
now. So when I walk out of this room with my head
held high I want you to know that 'Je comprends
tout', and we will go our ways with a jest on our lips,
and if our hearts ache now and then we will know we
were wise to finish when we did. No, don't look now
because I'm going to disappear.

37

Turn Back the Clock

Music by Richard Addinsell

Our lovely time
Was the loveliest time
I have ever known,
But swift as an arrow
Shot from a bow
Our lovely time has flown.

Turn back the clock
To when you stepped from the train,
Turn back the clock
And live the whole thing again.
All we have done together
Has been such fine fun
Time starts to mock at us,
Why can't we turn back the clock?
Our lovely time makes a mock of us,
Why can't we turn back the clock?

Our happy days
Were the happiest days
Need they fade away?
For yesterday's laughter
Lives in our hearts,
Our happy days were true.

Turn back the clock etc.

Someday

'Someday' was sung later on in 1959 in
Oranges and Lemons,
by Denis Martin and Sylvia Ashmore

*And this is the letter he left for me to read after he'd
gone overseas*

Tomorrow I'm going away
And so I want you to know
All the things I've never been able to say.

You have opened my eyes to beauty,
All you touch turns to magic for me,
Magic of music and stars in the night —
All these are alight, because of you, for me.

Some day, some dreamed of tomorrow,
Will find us together and there will be loveliness then
When I see you again.
Oh, my darling, count on it too
And soon, quite soon,
It's bound to come true.
Someday we'll have our happiness,
Someday.

END OF WARTIME LEAVE, 1943

Drifting

Music by Richard Addinsell

I dream I am drifting
Like a leaf blown in the breeze,
Way over the houses
And away over the trees
A lovely sensation of effortless grace
As I glide through space

I dream I am drifting
Like a seabird in the sky,
Lazily sailing with the wind
    whispering by

All of my worries
Simply vanish in the air
My true love loves me,
Not a shadow anywhere.

I fly high — high,
And waken to find
I've only been dreaming.

Travel Broadens the Mind

Oh, do come in. You must be the one who 'phoned from the Newspaper Office and wanted to hear how two Tulse Hill girls had done their bit in the war. Now, may I introduce you? This is my Auntie, Mrs Geddowes, with whom I live; and this is my great friend and the girl who went overseas with me to help entertain the troops, Doreen Le Mair. We've had many good laughs together, haven't we, Doreen? I expect she'll tell you all about it later on. And your name is . . . ?

Mr Pool.

Now, where will you perch, Mr Pool? Will you be quite comfy on the leather pouffe? It's Algerian — a trophy of our travels. How about a ciggy? No, I don't, thanks, because of — well — my voice. I've been at it ever since I was a tiny kiddy, haven't I, Auntie? And everyone said it would be a crime for me to do anything likely to impair my voice, so I've had to be just a wee bit strict with myself.

Well, you'd like to hear about the tour, wouldn't you? Statistics as follows: we were away for over two years, we visited fifteen countries and I sang the Ave Maria over six hundred times. I do all Deanna Durbin's numbers. Well, we started in West Africa.

It was *West* Africa, wasn't it, Doreen? Yes, and you

got the tom-tom for your friend's flat — he uses it as an occasional table. And from West Africa we went over to North Africa, and I shan't forget that in a hurry. I had to keep on singing 'The Holy City' for a Major in the Tank Corps who followed our show around until they took his tank away from him, foolish fellow.

Well, from North Africa we went over to Malta. That's an island, you know, so of course it's mainly Navy. Oh, it's quite a cheery spot.

Auntie, could you be a dear and slip into my Den for me and see if you can find that snap of me taken on the gun with the Admiral? I think it's with the others under the elephant bell.

I'd love you to see my Den sometime, Mr Pool. It's really rather sweet. All my own books and pictures. I'm a terrible bookworm. I curl up in there for hours and quite forget the world, it's awful. . . .

Well, from Malta we went over to Sicily, and there wasn't much in the shops there. And from Sicily we went over to Italy, and in Italy I had a big thrill in hearing *La Bohème* done in its native tongue. And while we were in Italy a Wing-Commander I got to know rather well made me sing Handel's *Largo* for him by moonlight in the Forum at Rome. Doreen played for me on the accordion.

Well, I don't know what I'd say was the most popular item on the programme, do you, Doreen? I suppose some might say my Ave, but I think I preferred Doreen's Drummerette Dance. It's a novelty number and she does it against a backcloth depicting a huge toy drum, and she wears just a little red, white and blue brassière and panties and a pillbox hat at a jaunty angle. It's very sophisticated, it's quite West End. The boys used to whistle like anything. I must admit they whistled at my Ave too, if I say it as shouldn't.

Well, from Sunny Italy we went over to Egypt, and in Cairo we were very much fêted and spoilt. I saw the Sphinx seven or eight times with different friends. And while we were in Cairo we managed to get our costumes freshened. You see, I only wore white in the show — it's more suitable for my type of song, isn't it? Just a very simple, white, draped gown.

Very simple, very draped.

Someone rather special said I put him in mind of a lily in it. But he was rather prejudiced. And he did have the most unusual gift of second sight. It was really very remarkable.

Well, I mustn't talk too much about myself because I know you want to hear about the tour. Well, we went across the desert and down to Basra, then over to India, Land of Magic and Mystery! Oh, and problems too. I heard all about the problems from a Brigadier I got to know up in Dacca, but I'd no idea till I read Beverley Nichols's little book just what really did go on out there. Oh, it's very worrying, I mean to say if you stop and think. I'm a terrible thinker, I can't stop thinking, I'm thinking all the time, it's awful.

Doreen, why don't you tell this nice person a bit about yourself? You know, you're not a bit like a newspaper man, Mr Pool you're so quiet. But then I do rattle on, don't I, and neither you nor poor Doreen can get a word in edgewise. I'll tell you about Doreen. Not only does she dance but she plays the accordion as well, gipsy style, up and down the stage, or, when we're in canteens, in and out of the tables — when they've got the tables. Oh, it's a lovely gift. I wish I had it.

43

With me it's rather different. I think it must be the music. They seem to more or less put me on a pedestal. I don't know why. . . .

No, I don't think we had any unusual incidents. Well, we did get to know rather a rich Rajah up in the hills. He called me Little Flower and gave me an electric iron. I think he'd been to Cambridge or somewhere like that.

Oh yes, we saw our boys everywhere we went. They looked marvellous — lovely and sunburnt. I think they'd like to get back though, judging by what they said.

Oh, there's Auntie tinkling for elevenses. That's a temple bell she's tinkling. A Chindit gave it to me. Would you like some elevenses?

Good, and I can show you my Den, and I'll make Doreen talk. I'll make her tell you about the time we were in Greece and she had to do a tap dance on the Parthenon.

SIGH NO MORE, 1945

44

Oh, Mr du Maurier!

Music by Richard Addinsell

I have stood for Mr Millais, and I've sat for Madox
    Brown;
I've been graceful for D.G. Rosetti, in a florissy-
    Morrisy gown.
I seem to delight each pre-Raphaelite, Mr Holman
    Hunt takes me to lunch;
I've been done in half-tones by Sir Edward Burne-
    Jones, but
I've never appeared in *Punch*.

Oh, Mr Du Maurier! Why cannot I be
One of your wittier women like the lady on page
    two three?
There may be prettier women, *plus grande
    dame* maybe;
But they couldn't find one more Du Maurier, or
    more drawrier than me.

The Rossettis read me poems at the house in
    Cheyne Walk;
And Lord Tennyson flattered me lately, in a
    Lordly-Maudly talk.

I seem to incite the writers to write, Mr Ruskin
   admires my mind;
Mr Browning finds I'm like a mystical rhyme, Du
   Maurier only is blind.

Oh, Mr Du Maurier! I would like to know
On what your neglect of me hinges, for it hurts
   my vanity so.
I've got the face and the fringes, so I say,
   pianissimo,
I would sit for you, dear Du Maurier, *con amorier
   molto*.

Oh, Mr Du Maurier! Perhaps I'm out of date.
Time flies when one isn't counting at a beastly
   Priestley rate.
The years must have gone on mounting, and
   now, I estimate
That I'm seventy years, dear Du Maurier, what
   a bore-ier too late.

The Countess of Coteley

Music by Richard Addinsell

Knowing Ed Sullivan's love of contrasts I should not have been so surprised when he asked me to do this number on his programme. I sang and spoke the piece, dressed to the nines in a tiara with an order ribbon across my white satin gown, standing in a gold frame, as the subject of a 1910 portrait by John S. Sargent. Ed said it was just the thing for his Sunday night programme as a contrast to Elvis Presley (who was also in the programme). It was a mild piece of social comment. Perhaps it went against the mood of the time. Labour had just swept into power and to suggest that there was still some worth in the old order may have seemed risky, but I was ready to chance my arm and I'm glad I did. 'Coteley' was not everyone's favourite number, but it had its enthusiasts and one of them was Oscar Hammerstein who thought I should write an entire musical on the same subject.

The Countess of Coteley!
Wife of the Eleventh Earl,
Mother of four fine children,
Three boys and a girl.
Coteley Park in Sussex,
Strathrar on the Dee,
Palace Gardens, Kensington,
Aged thirty-three.

Look at the Countess of Coteley!
Here you see her when
She was at her zenith and the year was nineteen-ten.

Is she happy, would you guess?
The answer to that question is, more or less.

For she's never heard of Hitler, and she's never
    thought of war,
She's got twenty-seven servants, and she could get
    twenty more.
She never sees a paper, and she seldom reads a book,
She is worshipped by her butler, tolerated by her
    cook.
And her husband treats her nicely, and he's *mostly* on
    a horse,
While the children are entirely in the nursery of
    course.
So no wonder she is happy — she's got nothing else to
    do.
O, no wonder she is happy, for she hasn't got a clue,
To the future that is waiting, and the funny things
    she'll do
About . . . thirty-seven years from now.

When you see her in this flashback it is rather hard to
guess
That she'll be a sort of typist in the W.V.S.
She will learn to woo her grocer: she won't have a
cook to woo,
But a Czechoslovak cleaner may pop in from twelve
to two.
Speaking worldlily she'll dwindle. She will change her
book at Boots,
And lecture on Make-do-and-Mend to Women's
Institutes.
She will lose the Earl quite quietly, and her young
will leave the nest,
She never knew them very well, so that is for the
best.
And Coteley, Strathrar, Kensington will vanish with
the rest
About . . . thirty-seven years from now.

Now the National Trust has Coteley, which is quite a
handy dodge,
And she'll make a flat of part of what was once the
keeper's lodge.
She will seldom dress for dinner, she will dote on
Vera Lynn,
She will take in the *New Statesman*, but she won't be
taken in.

Here you see her in this flashback looking decorative
but dumb,
For she hasn't got an inkling of the jolly days to
come!
Though the distances she'll travel are incredible to
tell,

And the quandaries she'll cope with will be absolutely
    hell,
She'll emerge in Forty-seven having done it rather
    well!

Will she be happy, would you guess?
The answer to that question is . . . Y—e—s.

TUPPENCE COLOURED, 1947

Artist's Room

The scene takes place in the artist's room at the back of a concert hall where a piano recital has just happened and now various friends and acquaintances of the pianist come round to see him.

First, a pair of front stalls

Delia darling, he's got such a crowd around him. Don't let's push. Let's sit here for a minute. I'm absolutely exhausted after all that lovely, lovely music. I thought he played quite well, didn't you? But I still think that Beethoven is a tiny bit on the long side. He does go on so, Beethoven, bless his heart. Just when you think he's finished the entire thing starts again. I think I prefer delicious little bits of Debussy.

But I'm glad it was such a success. He's such a nice little man. Yes, I know him quite well. You know Milly Medlow Sims? Well, she has three Sunday evenings and one goes in and one sits on lovely, lovely chairs and listens to lovely, lovely music, and she knows a lot of amusing people ... oh, actors and writers, musicians and MPs and things ... and she's so intelligent about it. I mean if there is somebody there who plays the piano she goes up to them very casually and she says: 'Now look, I'm not going to be a bully

51

because I hate bullies. But there is my piano and we are all dying to hear you play, so if you feel in the least like it, do play.' And they usually do.

No darling, she doesn't pay them. The whole thing is just great fun. I mean it couldn't be more informal. One goes on talking.

I don't know how anyone manages without music in their life. Well, it's just part of me, I think. I just sit there and let the whole thing pour over me. I think the reason I don't like Beethoven is that he just doesn't pour.

Look darling, the crowd is getting thinner. I think that if I was to push a little I could have a tiny word in his ear, and he'd never forgive me if I didn't Don't you bother to come. It's just one of those things one has to do and it won't take a second.

Excuse me if I push in front of you. I am in rather a rush.

Do forgive me, I must push past you.

Hello, I can't tell you how heavenly it was. It could not have been more heavenly. I don't know if you remember but we did meet with Milly Medlow Sims in the dim dark ages and I felt I simply had to come and tell you how heavenly it was. Look, I do wish you'd ring me up some time. I'm in the book and you could come round to my house some time and we'll all make music madly together. Do, do, do that. It's a promise. I can't tell you how heavenly it was. Absolutely heavenly . . .

Come on Delia.

A group of balcony tickets

Hello. I said I'd come, didn't I?

Jolly well played! Absolutely smashing! We all

thought so.

May I introduce you? Mummy, you know.

This is Mrs Maxwell, and Colonel Maxwell. And Barbara Maxwell and Joan Maxwell. And Ian Maxwell. I think that's about the lot! Oh no, Michael Maxwell! Sorry, Mike!

Well, we all thought it was absolutely marvellous.

I think I liked the encore best. Yes, I have heard it before.

I think I heard Eileen Joyce do it, only she does it quicker!

I say, we are by way of going back to the Maxwell's for some food and it isn't frightfully far actually, just the other side of London. Thurloe Square. There'll be heaps of food and a very warm welcome if you happened to feel like it. But perhaps you aren't hungry. I expect you're jolly tired after all that practising and you aren't in the least hungry, but if you did feel like it just leap into a taxi and turn up. We won't expect you, but if you did come it would be marvellous. I expect we'll have some more music. Old Mike plays the squeeze box! And anyway there would be a wonderful welcome for you. But don't make up your mind now. Don't take any ghastly decisions! It's so awful to be trapped and feel you must come, so just leave it free. IF you feel like coming just come and if you don't, don't. But it would be lovely if you did . . .

All right, Mummy — I'm coming —

A pair of complimentary tickets

There he is, Mrs Millstone! Well, you said you'd go in and say why Mrs Hill couldn't use the seats. You got your glasses? And the programme? That's right. It's nice to see what you've been listening to and you can show it to Eric, can't you? And Mrs Hill. It was very nice of her to give us the seats and they were lovely seats. I like to be able to see their faces.

Oh, I think singing is different, dear. I mean any person can sing if they've got the voice, but the piano is different. I always think there is something different about the piano.

He got quite warm, didn't he?

You have got your glasses? That's right.

I should think he's tired after all those notes. I know I am.

No dear, I wasn't listening all the time. I was thinking some of the time.

I was wondering if that letter has come from Con. She always writes it to me on the Tuesday and I get it on the Wednesday. You know if she's written it on the Tuesday.

She is a nice woman. Pity about her tooth.

I was just thinking she would have liked that Swedish piece he played.

Yes, he did dear. He played a Swedish piece. I heard it with me own ears. It's in the programme. Let's look. Swedish ... Swedish ... where have you got to Swedish. Oh ... Spanish dance. Isn't that funny? I saw Swedes! Never mind. Comes to the same thing in the end. Foreigners.

Oh, look dear, we can have a word with him now.

Come on, don't be shy. You look nice in that hat, you'd be surprised. Come on.

How do you do? I'm Mrs Pelly and this is my friend Mrs Millstone, and Mrs Hill said she is ever so sorry she couldn't use the seats because of her chest. But it's been a lovely outing for us. It's always nice to get up to London again. Any excuse.

And finally, one single top balcony unreserved

I'm afraid you don't know me.
  I just want to say, Thanks, MOST awfully.
  Thanks, M—O—S—T awfully.

TUPPENCE COLOURED, 1947

Odyssey

One of my two new monologues was a view of England, in those austerity days just after the war, seen by a visiting American woman from the limited vantage-point of the Dorchester Hotel.

The scene takes place in a very rich apartment of a very rich lady living in New York City.
Time: Very much in the present [1947].

Darling Johnny, how divine to see you and Chattie, darling, how divine. Come right in.

Dimitri.

Isn't he divine? He is the best White Russian butler in the whole of New York. I got him in Paris. He doesn't speak one word of English but it's very good for me because it makes me use my French. But, come right on in and sit down, because I can't wait to tell you about England.

It's ghastly! We got in last night. We were there for two entire weeks living perfectly typical British lives, so I mean I really do know what goes on there and it could not be more hideous.

To start with, we stayed, like they all do when in London, at the Dorchester, so I mean the whole thing is quite normal, and of course we talked to everybody everywhere we went and we went everywhere and we saw everybody. We saw Mabel Carthew and the Bolchesters and Freddy Wansworth, and Cissie Bolchester told us they are living in *one* wing of their house. Oh, I know it is an enormous one, Chattie; I think it has seventeen or eighteen bedrooms, but it is the principle of the thing. Freddy Wansworth said: 'Don't go to Scotland, you will be fools if you go to Scotland.' He said there are no grouse on the moors, no salmon in the rivers and nothing to kill. In the old days there used to be so much to kill and such divine people doing it.

You see, the thing is, they have got this Government that just isn't on their side. Oh yeah, Freddy is still in the House of Commons but no one listens to a word he says, and he gets back at night exhausted and hoarse from yelling. It's pathetic.

Oh merci, Dimitri.

Isn't he divine, and, Johnny, politically he is so sound. He is in favour of people having lots of money and I think he is so right. Well, in England it is no good if you have got it, you can't do a thing with it.

What are you going to drink, darling? Well, just help yourself.

Oh, my dear, over there, you stand in line; wherever you are going, whatever you are doing, you are standing in line. You have to take your turn and it can be very humiliating. One night we had nothing better to do and I said to Walthrop: 'How about going and seeing this Ballet you hear so much about.' So we went along to the place where they had it and we saw something very sordid. About the slums in Edinburgh someplace? And when we got outside afterwards the car we had ordered just never arrived. We could not get a taxi, we had to go right outside and stand in the open street, waiting in line for all of five minutes, waiting for a bus, and when it came it was going in the wrong direction. We had to start the whole thing all over again and on the second bus we got separated. They made Walthrop go upstairs and I was allowed downstairs, and I was terrified. Well, mercifully I was wearing a very simple little white chiffon dress from Mainbocher and my little sable jacket, but I might have been wearing anything. I had on some of that new perfume I got in Paris. It is called *Hell*. It is divine, and the man they have on the bus came right up to where I was sitting and said: 'Phew lady, you don't half pong lovely.' Well, I think maybe he did mean it nicely. I mean it may be a very pretty thing to say — only we just don't happen to know. But it was a hideous experience and I was nervous for days.

I swear I don't believe I would go to England if I was you.

Well, I mean it starts you thinking and what's the use of that? Johnny, I don't think it is wrong to have privilege as long as you pay for it. Do you?

TUPPENCE COLOURED, 1947

I Like Life

Music by Richard Addinsell

*I was asked to write another song, not this
time a comedy number but a straight song
to be sung as myself, and this turned out to
be a piece of personal philosophy called 'I
Like Life', set to one of Dick's prettiest
waltz tunes.*

When people ask me where are you heading?
What is life all about?
The answer, I suppose, Heaven only knows,
Even so, I can say without doubt:

I like Life, common or garden or what you will,
I get a thrill from it, still, I probably always will.
Even when I'm low as a snake, feel I'd like to jump
   in the lake,
I don't jump
Because I like it better the way things are,
Muddled and marvellous, yes, I far prefer things as
   they are,
I find I like life.

When I ought to be rushing to keep an appointment,
Ought to be looking alert in a shop,
When I ought to be planning the meals and preparing,

I'm standing and staring, I can't stop.
I'm listening in to conversations in queue and bus and
   train,
And even when I've been feeling abysmal I soon feel
   good again.
For I am a moron, an awful old bore on the subject
   contained in this refrain:

I like life, summer and winter and every day,
Whether it's gloomy or gay, November or rainy May,
Even when I'd rather be dead, feel I'd like to chop off
   my head,
I don't chop
Because I like it better the way things are,
Muddled and marvellous, yes, I far prefer things as
   they are.
I find I like, yes, I do like life!

TUPPENCE COLOURED, 1947

Going Abroad for the Hols

Telephone introduction

Hello, Peg. Can I come over? Is your mother in? Bother. Is she going out soon? Good, I've got something frightful to tell you. Something absolutely awful. I'll come over now.

Oh, Peg, thank goodness you're here. The most absolutely ghastly thing has happened. Mother's just told me we're going to *France* for the summer hols.

Isn't it awful? *Abroad*. The worst ghastly part is that we shan't be going to darling Sandy Bay.

I feel as if the whole of my life had sort of finished. There's no point in anything any more. No point in practising at tennis or diving or anything.

And I think it's so *disloyal* to the cottage we always take. It's such a heavenly cottage. No light — no running water, and the wind blows through all the rooms so it's like being out of doors all the time, and all we ever need there are thick jerseys and our macintoshes. Mum did all the cooking in lovely smelly oilstoves. Oh, it was such bliss!

And now we're going abroad.

Someone's gone and lent us a villa in the South of France, so we're going to take the car and drive there.

It's right on the sea and the sun shines every day and you can bathe four or five times a day if you want to. It's got a garden full of flowers, and grapes everywhere.

I shall hate it.

Daddy says the water's absolutely clear so you can see all the little fishes and shells and things in it, and there's a boat and a diving board and there's a super cook there, who is supposed to be terrific.

Are you going to Sandy Bay?

Gosh, you are lucky.

I don't suppose you'd want to come with us if Mum says I can ask anyone to stay? If you came we could sort of pretend we were at Sandy Bay — except there won't be any rain.

Oh Peg, isn't it awful?

Going *abroad* for the hols.

1948

Life and Literature

This number was first performed at a party given by Sir John Gielgud to the company at the Royal Shakespeare Theatre at Stratford-on-Avon in 1950.

I feel as if I'd known you for absolute ages instead of only half an hour. It was awfully clever of you to find such a lovely quiet place, even if it is a bit dark. Of course, in a way I do know you through your books, and when Alison said, 'Do come in on Friday because Lionel Pilgrim is going to be there,' I almost died. I said, 'Not *the* Lionel Pilgrim?' and she said, 'Yes.' I almost died.

Yes, I've read all your books. No, I haven't got them. I got them out of the library. They didn't actually have them, but they got them for me. Well, I think it's your honesty I admire so much. You know, the way you use rude words and that. And then you always have such original backgrounds. I never knew Edinburgh was like that. Oh, I've been through it on the way to places, but you know, it didn't seem like that.

Oh, I know what I thought was absolutely *marvellous*. You know that man in the book you wrote about Istanbul — *Sin is a Fair Flower* — well, I thought it was so marvellous the way you made him so harsh and evil, and so cruel to his wife — branding her and everything — and yet all the time, deep down, he was frightfully religious. I was awfully surprised when he became a nun — I mean a monk.

I say, you had a very unhappy childhood, didn't you? Oh, I just guessed. Well, you are Henry in *The Heart has no Womb*, aren't you? I thought so. Poor you. It must have been awful. I mean about your father, and then having to be a Wolf Cub when you couldn't believe in it. You know that bit in the disused gravel-pit where the girl taunted you? Well, I don't think, I *absolutely* understood it quite, though I thought it was awfully interesting. Frightfully clever.

Oh, I had a very happy childhood. Well, we lived in the country and I had a pony . . . and lots of cousins . . . and we played games, and had fun . . . and I used to scribble a bit. Poetry. I still do, actually. Oh no, it's no good at all. Absolutely hopeless. Well, Mummy thinks it's quite good, but I mean it *isn't*. Oh no, not love poems, more things like Spring, and Flowers . . . and Death.

My hair isn't in the least bit Greek! I just twist it up and it stays there. No, I couldn't possibly take it down. Because I should feel so frightfully silly. No, I couldn't possibly. I say, are you feeling hungry? I mean, we could go back to the buffet or something. No, I'm not in the least hungry. I love just sitting here and talking.

Don't be silly, my skin isn't in the least transparent. Do shut up.

I say, may I ask you something? Well, do you think that if a person is going to write about the sort of things you write about, do they have to actually experience all those things before they can write about them?

Oh. — Well then, I don't suppose I'll ever write

anything. Well, I live in the country, and absolutely *nothing* ever happens . . .

Oh, I'd love to come and have dinner with you one evening and talk about it. What fun!

May I bring Mummy?

PENNY PLAIN, 1950

Picture-Postcard

Music by Richard Addinsell

Before pin-up girls there were picture-postcard photographs of actresses on sale, and this lyric is about a showgirl in the 1914—1918 war. Skindles is the name of a riverside hotel at Maidenhead where young officers of the day took their girls. There is a legend that says no officer in the 'Blues' — the Household Cavalry — in those days was permitted to marry an actress.

I'm the picture-postcard that your Uncle Willy kept
In his wallet, till the very day he died.
I'm the picture-postcard that your Auntie Milly
   found
In your Uncle Willy's wallet,
When he dropped it on the ground.
How your Uncle Willy frowned!
How your Auntie Milly cried!
(For she was only a bride.)

He lied, of course. He tried, of course,
Denied he'd ever known me.
He sighed, of course, and cried, of course,
Pretended to disown me.

But I'm the picture-postcard that your Uncle Willy
   kept
In his wallet till the very day he died.
While awake or while he slept,
In his wallet, ever after,
Till the very day he died.

As a showgirl I played at the Palace
In the First War, long ago.
And he was a subaltern in the Blues,
And oh! he loved me so.
But he was already promised
To the Lady Millicent Platt,
And though it seemed a pity —
That was that.
We knew at the time it was Kismet;
It wouldn't have worked, you see,
For they don't marry actresses in the Blues —
So that was that for me.
But oh! the happiness, oh! the joy;
Even now the memory kindles,
Then we parted, broken-heartedly,
One summery Sunday at Skindles.

But I'm the picture-postcard that your Uncle Willy
   kept
In his wallet till the very day he died.
While awake or while he slept,
In his wallet ever after. Till the very day,
The very day,
The very day he died.
Do you wonder how I know?
Your Auntie Milly told me so.

PENNY PLAIN, 1950

Thought for Today

For the original, English version of this sketch, written in 1950 for 'Penny Plain', the speaker used the same bright South-of-England suburban voice as the W.I. lecturer in 'Useful and Acceptable Gifts'. When I went to Broadway for the first time in 1954 I re-wrote the monologue and changed the background and income group of the enthusiastic speaker. This American woman has houses on Long Island and in Maine, a farm in Virginia and an apartment (or maybe a duplex?) in Manhattan, the scene of the sketch. She frequently crosses the Atlantic. The long drawling vowel sounds I used for this woman once indicated immense wealth. The same vowel sounds are heard in her fluent French.

Lily, darling . . . How divine to see you. Come right on in.

Dimitri, voulez-vous apporter les drinks ici au librairie, toute suite. Oui, toutes les bouteilles. Isn't he divine, Lily? He's the only White Russian butler left in the whole of New York. I found him in Paris and he's so typical. Moody and depressing. Just the way the Russians used to be. So much more fun. But Lily, come and sit down. I can't wait to tell you what's

68

happened to me.

My dear, I am entirely different . . . Well, I am inside.

Lily, have you ever heard of Dr Pelting? My dear, you're going to. He is the most marvellous man in the whole world, and he knows the answer to everything.

Lily, you know how I worried? Oh, I mean I worried so I fell asleep all the time doing it . . . just talking to people or playing bridge . . . and I worried whether to go to California or get my hair cut. And I worried whether it was wrong to be so rich. But Dr Pelting says it isn't in the least wrong. He says it's fine to be rich.

You see he's made this marvellous discovery.

Lily, Dr Pelting's message to you, to me, to the whole world . . . is simply this:

Don't think.

Isn't it *exciting*? Oh, I know what you're going to say. What will happen if I don't think? And the marvellous answer is . . . Nothing! Because Earth Ray Thought Forces are going to think for you. It seems the earth is full of wonderful forces, but how to make contact?

Lily, where do we touch the earth most closely? Exactly . . . our feet. And what we get through our feet are Earth Ray Thought Forces.

I met him at Emily's. I'd had my face done, so I thought I might as well use it, and I put on a new little black dress I got at Balmain and some divine perfume called *Fiasco*, and honestly I didn't feel too unattractive. But this man came over to me, and he said, 'You need help,' and I said, 'How do you *know*?' and he told me he had been guided to me by Earth Ray Thought Forces. And he told me that these forces enter the body through the soles of the feet, and that's the way they influence the mind. And he said anybody can renew supplies if they will only stand in earth night and morning, if possible facing north.

I said to him, 'Look, sweetie, I can do that out in the country down at the farm in Virginia, but I cannot do it here in New York, on the eighteenth floor. And anyway I don't know which way north is.'

But he said, 'Look, all you have to do is get yourself a little tray, fill it with earth and stand in that.' And, he said, any passing Girl Scout will tell you which way north is.

He is a man of such vision.

Well, we went to the country that weekend, and I stood in earth every day, night and morning, even when it rained. I did it in a flower-bed, and it certainly felt as if I was facing north.

Well, when I'd gotten over a silly little chest cold I came back to New York, and I got myself a little tray, and I use it all the time. Walthrop says he doesn't know me any more. I tried to make him do it too, but you know he is so blind to his basic needs, and he says he gets all he wants in life from Benzedrine.

But I couldn't do without E.R.T.F. — Earth Ray Thought Force; and Eddie — Dr Pelting — comes in here on his way home sometimes, and we do it together on my little tray. Well, because two people make twice as much force. We just stand there and he takes my hands in his . . . he has enormous hands . . . and we say together:

From me to you, from you to me,
Let Earth Ray Thought Force pass
And benefit us both and take complete control.

Then we break contact . . . that means we let go of each other's hands and let E.R.T.F. take over.

No, he's not good-looking. He's . . . he's just very vital.

70

Lily, you must try it. You'll love it. Let's go find my little tray right now.

O merci, Dimitri . . . mettez les drinks ici, là, sur le piano. Oh, bon. Little cheesy things. *Merci. Non, c'est tout. Merci.*

You know, Lily, he's not as gloomy as he used to be. I wonder if he's been using my little tray . . . ?

PENNY PLAIN, 1950

Joyful Noise

Music by Donald Swann

Three lady choristers,
Members of the Royal Harmonic Society,
Singing eagerly, but with piety
All the Oratorio

Coming long distances to rehearse,
Fully familiar, chapter and verse,
With *all* the Oratorio.

Miss Clissold, Miss Truss, I'm Ivy Trembley,
From Raynes Park, Bayswater, Wembley.

Three lady choristers, silver voices all,
Some are sop, who sing on top,
And some are alt, who sing contralto
At the Albert Hall.

We sometimes sing in churches,
And at the BBC,
We sometimes sing *f,f,f,f,*
And sometimes *p, p, p.*
But we are at our happiest when we hear the call
To come and sing like anything
As long as it's Oratorio.

To come and sing like anything
As long as it's Oratorio,
How glorious the Glorio
All dressed in white with scorio
Encore — io,
In any Oratorio
At the Albert Hall

It may be rather gloomy, the audience may be thin,
But it is so nice and roomy to *rallentando* in
It may be like a gasworks with a greenhouse roof
    above it
And it may lack convenience but all the same we love
    it.
We do not mind the echo of a loud note when we
    strike it.
We let it go with might and main main
Then back it bounces once again
Again
Or even twice,
Or even twice,
Or even twice,
Or thrice again
Or thrice again
Or thrice again
Or thrice again
We really rather like it

We sit for all the solos, then graciously we rise
In one concerted movement, to everyone's surprise!
And it is most confusing when you have lost the way —
To hear your neighbour singing B while you are still
    on A.

We are not very musical, but we are very keen,
We practise every Thursday night quite close to
    Golders Green,
And some of us cannot sing much,
And some can't sing at all,
But how we love our outings to
— the Royal Albert Hall.

Teacher

originally performed by Diana Churchill

There are thirty-seven girls in the form I teach
And their average age is fourteen
Fourteen!
And already they are out of reach.

I can't seem to speak their language
And yet I remember so clearly, even now,
How clear it was to me then
And I knew I couldn't fail to make it clear to them.
That's why I thought it was right to become a teacher.

They aren't rude to me or anything.
Oh, no.
But I don't seem to influence them very much.
I hardly influence them at all.
I cannot seem to make them *see*
The magic that words have for me,
To show them how to find their own increasing
    heaven.
But you can't do that with thirty-seven
In a form
And the Fanshaw Street buses drowning every other
    word of

As You Like It
And no time to stop and discuss anything
With the work laid down to a timetable
And exams waiting at the end of every poem.

That teacher in *The Corn is Green* did it, though.
But that was in a village, wasn't it,
Forty years ago? —
Not in a classroom meant for eighteen desks
And holding thirty-seven —
Thirty-eight including mine —
And the mechanised roar from the open window
Of the projection room at the Pallidrome
Over the road
Coming in in a mixture of canned violins
And enormous blurred voices and guns.

I offer to lend them books,
My Oxford Book of English Verse, for instance;
To tell them about Keats and about the Brontës
But I don't get them interested,
And of course they don't want to learn
They want to earn,
And the cigarette factory at the far end of Darling
    Street
Is just waiting to swallow them up.
'Clean Congenial Work, Good Wages, Canteens,
    Music'.
It says so on the gate.

They tell me they want to be 'free'
And all I want to do is to set them free in a world
A little bit wider than Darling Street.

That teacher in *The Corn is Green*
Only opened the door to one boy as far as I know.
Still I haven't even done that, I don't believe.
Unless you could count Alison Weaver?
She and I used to talk about Walt Whitman
And when she left she went in for psychology
And wrote a poem that got into the *Observer*
But I didn't like it very much.
So I don't think you could count Alison Weaver.

I have got here thirty-seven essays to correct for
    tomorrow
On 'Why the Pen is Mightier than the Sword'
And they will all be awful
And there won't be any time to tell them why they
    are awful
Because we must get on with *Twelfth Night*
For the exam
And our bit of Fanshaw Street is being mended
Just outside the form-room window
By a lot of drills
And the Pallidrome is showing a film called *Wonder
    Wings*
And that means aeroplane engines from the
    projection room.
I think I will take a little poison with my cheese salad
    tonight.
But of course I won't.

ORANGES AND LEMONS, 1951

77

Tristram

Oh, Trevor. I'm so glad you're home. Something rather serious has happened. It's Tristram. No, no he's not ill — he's all right, don't fuss so. He's ten years' old and he's not a fool.

I don't know how to tell you.

I'm so ashamed really.

Well, you know how Sunday has always been a sort of sacrosanct day with us, hasn't it? I mean we always sleep late and Tristram gets his own breakfast and then cleans out the hamsters and the budgies and his bike, while we stay in bed with the Sunday papers.

Well, it's Monday today and I happened to notice that Mrs Hamster hadn't been cleaned out, nor had the budgies, and Tristram's bike was rusty. So I called him in and I said: 'You know we never question you about your jobs, you are absolutely free to do them when and as you want. But I don't think it's fair on Mrs. Hamster and the budgies, do you, to leave them so dirty.'

He agreed that it wasn't. He's so wonderful that way.

And I said: 'You have all Sunday morning, don't you?' and he said: 'No.' And I said: 'But that's what you do on Sunday mornings,' and he said no it wasn't. And then it came out.

Trevor, Tristram's been going to church.

Oh, it's so disappointing.

And the terrible thing is he likes it.

I simply don't understand it.

He's intelligent and balanced and we've been so careful ever since he was tiny never to confuse him in any way. When he asked me about God I always managed to change the subject and talk about other things. I'd say: 'Oh look, there's a caterpillar,' or, 'Would you like a wholemeal scone for tea?' and he was happy as a sand boy.

I can't get him to discuss church. All he says is: 'I like it.'

Do you know, he's been going for months and months.

He does Mrs Hamster and the budgies after school on Mondays. I never noticed.

I can't understand it.

No, he doesn't go with anybody. He goes by himself.

I'm afraid it will get out, you know. Everybody knows we are agnostics. I've said so often enough on the wireless and you write about it in your articles.

Do you think we could ask him not to say anything about it? I mean it could be his secret. He might like that. And he is quite fond of us so he won't want to let us down, will he?

You could talk to him, man to man, and appeal to him.

I suppose he'll grow out of it and I said so to him, but he just laughed and said: 'Poor old Mum.'

We mustn't question him. It's his problem.

But what a pity if he is going to make such a mess of his life while he's so young.

1952

Private Secretary

originally performed by Betty Marsden

Yes, Sir Edgar.
No, Sir Edgar.
I'll see to it, Sir Edgar.
I've made a note of it, Sir Edgar.
Yes, Sir Edgar.

That was Sir Edgar — Sir Edgar Plumgrove.
I am his private secretary and have been for years-
     without-end-amen.
I didn't come in till he was about half way to the top
     but I saw a lot of it happen.
He's a self-made man, of course.
From the North.
He ran errands for a grocer,
Then he served in the shop,
Then he rose to manage it,
Bought it,
Enlarged it,
Opened a branch in the next town,
Opened two — four — six — eight branches, etc. etc.
And became a big name in trade.
'PLUMGROVE'S — There's one in YOUR Town.'

He was very useful in the war.
Now he is known everywhere by everybody in every
    walk of life.
He lunches to meet the P.M., informally of course.
He drops in for a drink at the club, the pub or the Ritz,
Dines at Claridges to meet anyone you can think of,
And weekends with the aristocracy — the *Tatler* and
    Sketch aristocracy that is.
He keeps Lady Plumgrove in a 1910 Baronial Hall at
    Wimbledon.
She's used to it now and she's got a couple of
    sealyhams to blot up her affections and an Italian
    maid to worry about.
So she's all right.
And then there are two daughters,
And three grandchildren called Ronnie, Wendy and
    Pixie.
And I remember all their birthdays.
They're all right.

And then there's the Monarch of the Glen himself —
Sir Edgar P.
And I suppose he's all right,
But he's not very nice really,
Not when you know how he ticks.
I mean you can *see* him getting on still, even nów.
I must say he has the gift for it —
Upward ever upwards.
And he never overplays his power,
At least not in public.

'Look,' he says at Public Dinners with Ministers of
    the Crown
And Dukes and the influential present,
'Look, I'm only a grocer who's been lucky,
So don't listen to me.'

And they laugh and applaud and pat him on the back,
And he does very well out of it from sheer
   naturalness.

I know the act rather well: all the variations on the
   theme.
The Jolly Eddie Plumgrove — this is good at the
   Savage Club:
The simple Unspoiled Giant — this is good with
   hostesses:
The Rough Northerner with the quizzical look —
This is splendid all round everywhere, on TV in
   particular.
He switches on the styles like lights and does it
   damned well.

The funny part is that he knows I know all this
And it worries him a bit,
So he takes it out on me in little ways.
Keeps me late when he knows I have tickets for a
   theatre,
And makes me change my holiday at the last minute.
Oh, he has an unerring instinct for petty cruelties
And uses them as if he hadn't any idea what he was
   doing.
But he knows all right!
And he knows that I know.
But what he doesn't know, though,
Is that for all these weary, wasted years
I've been in love with him,
And what is more
He never will know.
He's never going to have that little bit of power.

Yes, Sir Edgar.
At once, Sir Edgar.

AIRS ON A SHOESTRING, 1952

Women at Work 1

Here are three characters that I rather loosely call Women at Work, and the first of these is at work in one of those very small antique-cum-interior decorator's shops.

Antique Shop

Oh, do come in. How very sweet of you to come and see my terrible little dump. Well, it *is* rather fun, isn't it. Micky . . . Micky, Mrs Medlow Sims has angelically come to see us. MRS MEDLOW SIMS . . . he is inside a grandfather clock, Mrs Medlow Sims. It's rather a beautiful one we picked up for nothing — Micky is turning it into a tiny little television set. Oh, Micky . . . Mrs Medlow Sims, this is Micky Tidwell, my partner in crime. He does all the hard work and I just encourage from the sidelines.

Oh, it's true, Micky.

Well, I think it's very sweet of you to say so.

Mrs Medlow Sims, are you looking for anything special or would you like to browse? No, do browse — I always think it's so maddening when one goes into a shop and people try to sell one something, so I couldn't be more sympathetic and I shall expect you to browse and browse to your heart's content. Only, do be a little careful of your stockings. We are so terribly congested in here and one does so hate ladders, doesn't one? No, do go anywhere. Just make yourself at home and forget I'm here. I'll just be here.

Oh, aren't they fun. Antlers. Well, we think that is probably a moose; and that is probably a stag. I don't know whether you are at all amused by antlers, but we're rather besotted with them here and, as you see, Micky does such amusing things with them . . . painting them with luminous paint and then covering them with sequins. And, you know, not only are they madly pretty but they're madly practical as well. Oh, you can have one in your bathroom and put your *peignoire* and your bath-towel and your bath-cap on it, and then you can have another in your kitchen and put your entire *batterie de cuisine* on it — all the pots and pans and kettles . . . oh, no, perhaps it wouldn't do for Scotland.

I wonder — are you at all amused by wall papers? Oh, yes we're besotted with them here. No, we haven't actually got any, but we've got this little man in Paris and he flies over and he gets to know you and then he flies back to Paris and then he designs the paper specially for *you*. He's done the most fabulous one for the Cleestones, have you seen it? Well, the whole thing is a design of hands. There are happy hands and sad hands and frightened hands and clenched fists. I can't tell you how exciting it is. Well, they are sort of grey hands on a kind of khaki background. Oh dear, you prefer stripes? Well, I rather feel as if I'd *had* stripes. Well, you know you get home at the end of a long and exhausting day and there they are! Still going up and down. But I expect you are quite right about stripes.

Oh, isn't that a pretty little chair? I'm so glad you noticed it because it happens to be my favourite thing in the shop. You have got lovely taste. Do come round here and see it ... be a little careful of the stuffed crocodile. They are so sharp, aren't they?

Well, we think it must have been a theatre stall. Well, you see it is red velvet and it has that number there and the darling little ash-tray at the back. I think we said ten pounds — Micky ... what did we say for the little red chair? ... Nine pounds nineteen and six. Oh, you are so right, we did. (I'm so ashamed I'm not very good at pennies but I must pull myself together because the money side is so important in a shop, isn't it?) It's nine pounds nineteen and six — Yes, it *is* a lot. But it's such fun and I always feel we have to pay more for fun.

I wonder — are you at all amused by hip baths? — you know, those tin enamel affairs one's grandmother sat and washed in before her bedroom fire. Well, I'm afraid we really are rather besotted about hip baths here, and Micky does the most amusing and really rather naughty things with hip baths. Oh, you *must* come and see them. We keep them outside — in a sort of — place. Oh, the things he does with them! Sometimes he plants the entire hip bath with little tiny lettuces — I'd never have thought of it, would you? And then sometimes he fills the hip bath with water and you have gold fish and little toy boats. The whole thing is very *maritime* and *so* welcoming in the front hall. But I think my favourite thing is his idea for the drawing room. You hurl a whole mass of lovely coloured cushions into a hip bath and then you can get in and curl up with a good book.

Would you like to try?

Oh do —

Micky — make way — make way — Mrs Medlow Sims is dying to curl up.

JOYCE GRENFELL REQUESTS THE PLEASURE, 1954

Women at Work 2

Behind the Counter

Of course, it was all white. She got this sweet-heart neck line with a little fullness over the bust and then she got all these little buttons going up the front. There must of been two — two and a half dozen little *tiny* satin-covered buttons going all the way up the front. I did like those little buttons.

(I won't keep you a moment.)

But I didn't like the head-dress. Well, it was silver leafs like this and then she got heather here. Well, it's hard on the face, heather. Of course, going up the aisle she got her veil all over her face, you couldn't see who it was, might of been anybody. Oh! it was a lovely veil. I'm not saying it wasn't a lovely veil, because it was a lovely veil.

(I won't keep you a moment.)

You know that sister-in-law. The one lives in a caravan on the main road by-pass? Well, *she* lent it her. It's a lovely thing. *All* over lace with a great lace border all round it. Looks like spiders made it and, of course, when she come down the aisle she'd thrown it back and you could see who it was and she looked quite nice. I was surprised. And in the sweet-heart neckline she got a little fine chain round her neck with a little blue drop on it! Something borrowed, something blue, see. And she was carrying —

(I beg your pardon, I won't keep you a moment.)

She was carrying white crysanths and green rosemary leafs because of the well-known saying — 'Here is rosemary that is for old memories' — You've heard that, dear. Yes, you're the one that likes poetry — 'Here's rosemary, that's for old memories'.

(I'm sorry I can't help you, it's just time for my tea break.)

JOYCE GRENFELL REQUESTS THE PLEASURE, 1954

Women at Work 3

Writer of Children's Books

The scene takes place in the Book Department of a large store where an author has been autographing copies, and now she is going to talk to her young readers.

Hullo, boys and girls. I was so pleased when you asked me to come along and tell you how I write my books for children. Well, of course, the answer is — I don't. No, my books write themselves for me.

I think we are all Little Ones at heart, aren't we, grown-ups? Yes, even the Growly Bear Daddies at the back! And I don't believe I have ever grown up, and I think perhaps that's my secret. That, and the fact that kiddies come first with me.

Well, as you know, children, I write lots and lots of books for you and this is how I set about it. First of all I go upstairs to my Hidey Hole — well, this is really just a great big upstairs workroom but I like to call it my Hidey Hole. I pin a notice on the door and it says: 'Gone to Make Believe Land'. This is just my way of saying: 'Please don't come and bother me because a book is writing itself for me and we mustn't disturb it, must we?'

Then I put a clean white sheet of paper in my typewriter and I sit down in front of it and I close my eyes. And what do I see? I see a rambling old house in Cornwall. And I hear seagulls — and I see children — one — two — *three* children scrambling up the cliffs because they are very nearly late for tea, and their names are Jennifer-Ann, and Robin-John, and the little one is called Midge — because he is the littlest one. (Oh yes, he has a proper name. It's Anthony Timothy Jeremy Michael and he doesn't like porridge — but we won't tell anyone, will we?)

And I sit there and I type and I type, and as I do so I learn all about Jennifer-Ann's unruly mop of red curls and her way with hedgehogs. And about Robin-John, who is more of a fish than a boy — you should see him dive from the top diving board. And all about their father — kindly, overworked, sunburned, twinkling Dr Merryweather.

Then all of a sudden it's dinner time and I rub my eyes and I find myself back in my Hidey Hole — and look! — a great pile of typed pages on the table beside me. They must have written themselves while the story told itself to me. And so I go on till a book is made. And then I start another one.

This time it's a rambling old house in Yorkshire, and I hear sheep bells and I see children — three children — and their names are Sara-Mary, Jonathan-Christopher, and the little one is called Tiddler — because he is the littlest one. It's always the same with me.

No, I never re-write and I never read what I have written. But you children do, millions and millions of you children do, and that is my great joy. And it is my husband's great joy, too. He has given up his work to encourage mine. We have made Hidey-Holes for each of our five children so that they, too, may learn to let books write themselves for them and my husband has his own Hidey-Hole where he adds up.

Well, I think it is time I got back to my Hidey-Hole, don't you?

JOYCE GRENFELL REQUESTS THE PLEASURE, 1954

The Music's Message

Music by Richard Addinsell

*On the Good Friday visit I found Walter de
la Mare, taking a day off in bed, in his blue-
panelled bedroom wearing blue pyjamas
with a red-and-blue silk handkerchief loosely
knotted under his collar like a cowboy's
scarf. After tea with hot-cross-buns he asked
for news of the show's progress, and I
described a new number, 'The Music's
Message', and did it for him — with move-
ments — in a corner of his room. It's a dotty
sort of song, sung by an earnest, ungraceful,
over-age schoolgirl type who joins a class in
search of 'the rhythms of the earth and sea
and sky'. The teacher tells her to listen
carefully and see what message the music
has for her. 'You must listen and listen and
listen, my dear.' (I stood still, listening
hard.) 'But the music said only one thing in
my ear: "You're a horse." '*

*Like a child W.J. said: 'More, please,'
and because I loved the opportunity of
showing off to him I did half the programme
and hoped I wasn't staying too long.*

On the back of a literary weekly
Under' 'Personal' I read it, just by chance.
It was meant for me to see, 'twas intended it should
  be,
Or I thought so from that first haphazard glance.
'Yours,' it said, 'the rhythms of the earth and sea and
  sky.'
'Learn,' it said, 'to dance the natural nature way.
Let the music through, find the inner you.
Two minutes' walk from Paddington Station, join our
  group today.'

So I went then and there and enrolled
And this is what I was told:
'Learn to loosen, loosen, loosen, loosen,
Bend to the music, just give way.
Go with the music where it takes you,
Don't be afraid if it leads you astray.
Listen to the music, get its message,
Learn to hear what the music will say,
Listen, listen, listen, listen,
Hark to the music and dance away.'

I stood where I was and relaxed as I should.
I waited and waited the message to hear.
I listened and listened, but hark as I would
The music said only one thing in my ear:
'You're a horse,' said the music, 'a great white horse
And you gallop and gallop and gallop the course,
And you leap and you leap and you whinney and
  neigh,
And you gallop and gallop and gallop away.'

'Rest,' said the teacher, 'Now listen anew.
You must learn to loosen or nothing comes through.'

So 'Loosen, loosen, loosen, loosen,
Bend to the music, just give way.
Go with the music where it takes you
Don't be afraid if it leads you astray.
Listen to the music, get its message,
Learn to hear what the music will say,
Listen, listen, listen, listen,
Hark to the music and dance away.'

'Rest,' said the teacher, 'Now listen my dear,
What is the musical message you hear?'
'You're *still* a horse,' said the music, 'a great white
    horse,
And you gallop and gallop and gallop the course,
And you leap and you leap and you whinney and
    neigh,
And you gallop and gallop and gallop away.'

JOYCE GRENFELL REQUESTS THE PLEASURE, 1954

Three Brothers

Music by Richard Addinsell

I had Three Brothers,
Harold and Robert and James,
All of them tall and handsome,
All of them good at games.
And I was allowed to field for them,
To bowl to them, to score:
I was allowed to slave for them
For ever and evermore.
Oh, I was allowed to fetch and carry for my
    Three Brothers,
Jim and Bob and Harry.

All of my brothers,
Harry and Jim and Bob,
Grew to be good and clever,
Each of them at his job.
And I was allowed to wait on them,
To be their slave complete,
I was allowed to work for them
And life for me was sweet,
For I was allowed to fetch and carry for my
    Three Brothers,
Jim and Bob and Harry.

Jim went out to South Africa,
Bob went out to Ceylon,
Harry went out to New Zealand
And settled in Wellington.
And the grass grew high on the cricket-pitch,
And the tennis-court went to hay,
And the place was too big and too silent
After they went away.

So I turned it into a Guest House,
After our parents died,
And I wrote to the boys every Sunday,
And once a year they replied.
All of them married eventually,
I wrote to their wives, of course,
And their wives wrote back on postcards —
Well . . . it might have been very much worse.

And now I have nine nieces,
Most of them home at school.
I have them all to stay here
For the holidays, as a rule.
And I am allowed to slave for them,
To do odd jobs galore,
I am allowed to work for them
And life is sweet once more,
For I am allowed to fetch and carry for the
    children of
Jim and Bob and Harry.

Hostess

Music by Richard Addinsell

When Mama gave a dinner for twelve
She rested all day long,
She rested all day long.

Oh, she ordered the meal
And directed the cook,
She ordered the flowers and took a last look
At the table.
But
She rested all day long,
She rested all day long.

Down below in her kitchen kingdom
The cook, Mrs Cooper, reigned supreme.
Down below in her kitchen working miracles
With butter
                sugar
                        and cream.
Ordering the kitchen maid called Maisie,
Ordering the scullery girl called Flo,
Keeping everybody in her kingdom
Hurrying to and fro.

Down below in his butler's pantry
The grand Mr Harrison reigned.
Down in his butler's pantry lording it
Over the young persons
He had trained.
Ordering the parlour maid called Beatrice,
Ordering the pantry boy called Jim,
Keeping everybody in his kingdom
Running around for him.

When Mama gave a dinner for twelve
She rested all day long,
She rested all day long.

Up above in her nursery kingdom
Nanny contrived to quiet her flock.
Up above in the nursery seeing
That the rocking horse didn't rock.

Gloomily the schoolgirls in the school room
Tidily in French the menus write
For their parents' dinner party
Later on that night.

When Mama gave a dinner for twelve
She rested all day long,
She rested all day long . . .

I'm only just home from the office.
Surely that clock can't be right!
I've only an hour to do it in
And we're giving a dinner tonight!

JOYCE GRENFELL REQUESTS THE PLEASURE, 1954

Daughter and Mother

Oh, Mummy, you don't understand. I've been thinking an awful lot about you and Daddy, now that you're both so old. Well, you're forty. Well, thirty-eight, then. Anyway, quite old — and you don't understand life any more. You see, Mummy, you married Daddy when you were frightfully young and you've been perfectly happy ever since, so no wonder you don't understand, because you've never suffered. I think it's rather pathetic really. Well, you don't like noise, and you think people ought to eat regular meals, and you don't understand about Art or anything. You and Daddy both think that if a person's going to do anything, they've got to learn *how* to do it, and then to work and work *hard*.

That's a frightful thing to say.

You see, you don't understand. Look — it's miles harder *not* to work than to work. Eric Witzler says that it's absolutely wrong to work, work is the coward's way out. And he says a creative artist must learn to starve if necessary.

No, he's the one who finished the cheese at supper on Sunday.

I suppose you think it's easy to paint a picture entirely solid blue. Well, it isn't. It takes hours and hours of concentration and discipline. It took Eric

98

three whole days before he ever *touched* the canvas, and absolutely *everyone* thinks it's the most exciting picture they ever saw in their whole lives. Well — everyone. Well — Esmond and Peggy and me.

Eric has such a tragic life. Well, he has to live at home with his family, and do you know he isn't allowed to play the gramophone or the radio after ten o'clock at night. You see, you *don't* understand. You and Daddy think it's awful to have the gramophone on all the time. But everyone up at the Universities do all their most complicated maths and science and that sort of thing with the radio and gramophones full on the whole time. Because it's the *only* way to concentrate.

And another thing, you think it's awful when I lie on the sofa and telephone someone for an hour.

But it's normal, Mummy.

I don't know how to say this without hurting your feelings, but you know last Saturday at Uncle Jim's? Well, you know the way we all played tennis? Well, I don't think you and Daddy ought to have beaten people so much younger than yourselves. George Pasby and Eleanor Dill are supposed to be frightfully good, and you kept sending them balls they couldn't take, and they didn't like it. And lobbing is frightfully old fashioned.

And I don't think you and Daddy ought to dance so sort of — well — enthusiastically — like you did at the Wilsons'. I mean, everyone was staring at you. You looked as if you were enjoying it.

Well, you ought not to of.

Look, Mummy, don't feel you've got to keep up with us. You've had a frightfully long life, and you must be tired. Are you going out tonight?

I just wondered. Nothing. I only asked.

Well, I wondered if you were going to wear your new jacket? Well, I mean, if you didn't actually want it, perhaps I could sort of borrow it.

Well, I just thought — Mummy, you're laughing at me!

JOYCE GRENFELL REQUESTS THE PLEASURE, 1954

Ballad

Music by Richard Addinsell

This is a ballad that tells the tale
Of the Dowager Duchess of L.
Who lives alone in the South of France
With her maid in a quiet hotel.

The scene is set in the Hotel Blanche,
The residents all are there;
The Dowager Duchess, cool and aloof,
Gets up from her wicker chair.

The Dowager Duchess cuts the cake,
'Tis her seventy-ninth birthday.
The diamond rings on her fingers spin
As she waves the years away.

'You'd never know to see me now,'
She cries, and her eyes are wild,
'That I was a servant long ago,
When I was a country child.

We lived by the river between the hills
And the Duke came there to fish.
I worked at the Castle all that year
At my sainted mother's wish.

My hair was as red as a fox, they say,
My eyes — he said they were green.
The moon was high and he was fair
And I was seventeen.

Our child was born one lonely night
And I was filled with joy,
And when the Duke returned in Spring
I showed to him the boy.

He turned as still as stone, and then
He said "We'll married be."
I did not know for twenty years
He had never cared for me.

The Duke was ever kind to me,
But when our son was grown
He said 'Now I am leaving you
And you will be alone.

The one I left to marry you
Is waiting still and free.
You have my name, my wealth, my house:
She nothing wants but me.'

I never saw his face again,
He died across the sea.
I do not know her name, nor if
She ever looks on me.'

'And now,' the Dowager Duchess said,
'I'm far too old to care.'
But she was pale as any ghost
When she went up the stair.

            JOYCE GRENFELL REQUESTS THE PLEASURE, 1954

Visitor

I am never quite certain whether this speaker is Dutch or Scandinavian; possibly Dutch with a Scandinavian mother. She travels a great deal with her high-powered businessman husband. The scene is yet another crowded cocktail party, where, of course, there is nowhere to sit. (For the American season in 1955 I wrote an American version of this sketch.)

Is dis not a smeshing cocktail party? I am so fond for a cocktail party. I sink is so nice to say hello and goodbye quick, and to have little sings for eating is so gay. Is always quite noisy and nowhere for sitting.

Yes, ve are here in London vis my husband. My husband is having business associate here in London, so ve are coming to London — and to Oslo, Copenhagen, Amsterdam, Paris — all over, and everywhere dere is a cocktail party. Most kind.

You are knowing Lady Hetting? She is a tall, sin Englis lady, and ven I am here two year ago Lady Hetting is most kind for me. Ve are making a sightsee together. Oh, ve are seeing Piccadiddly, and ve are seeing some modern art works at de Tate Gallery and ve are going to de Ideal Homes Exhibition. Lady Hetting is good for cooking. I am for bringing her a little gift horse. Is a chipple chopper. A chipple chopper? Oh, dis is a little gedget knife for cutting up celery. I sink she vill find him most useless.

Hello, how are you? I am smeshing vell senk you. You have see Lady Hetting? No, not yet. Tata just now.

Senk you, I would like somesing for eating. Vat is det? No senk you.

You are from London? Oh, you are from Cardiff. Det is nice. I was once in Scotland.

Senk you? Oh, I would like somesing for eating. Vat is det? No senk you.

Oh, Mrs Antrobus! I am so happy for seeing you again. May I present here is a nice gentleman from Scotland. Dis is Mrs Antrobus from God-alming in Surrey. How is Mr Antrobus? And you are still heving det little cat? You know ve are always laughing and talking about dis little cat from Mr and Mrs Antrobus. Is a most intelligent amusing little animal. You remember your little cat? Oh, I sought it was you was heving det little cat? Are you sure? A little cat vis a vite under? Vell it vas dis little cat was sneezing in rhythm to de music of Brahms. He is not sneezing for Mozart, not for Beethoven, Shostakovich, Chopin. No, no, only Brahms, and ven you vas going to de piano dis little cat vas for sneezing. Oh, you have no piano and no little cat? Oh, so sad.

I sink it vas a little cat from London, but ve are many places all over — ve are in Buenos Aires, in Melbourne, in Slough, all over. Ve are always somevere. So tiring.

Hello, how are *you*? I am sensational, senk you. No, I do not yet see Lady Hetting. I sink she is not coming. She is here? Vere? O dere, in de doorvay in de purple dress vis die Mexican jewellery. Hoo, hoo. Oh I am *so* heppy for seeing your jolly old face again.

Yes, ve vould like somesing for eating. Vat is dose?
Senk you. I vill try . . .
    Is dere an ashtray?

JOYCE GRENFELL REQUESTS THE PLEASURE, 1954

Regular partners you see.
Hers is a good one just like she is,
Mine dances more like me.

Both girls pull up brassières downstage right.
Waltz.
Paddy advances and by-passes Joyce. Joyce shakes
Irv's hand and dances. Joyce watches him, eyes glued
throughout waltz sequence which she does with Irv.
Not well. At the end she shakes Irv's hand again.
When Paddy does an elaborate lift with Beryl, Joyce
breaks from Irv and does a small solo spin. Irv is
ashamed. Paddy finally lifts Beryl and he staggers
with her downstage left. Joyce and Irv come close to
watch and Joyce says:

Oh Freda, you don't 'alf do it lovely.

(Joyce and Irv dance to and fro, just walking, in ensu-
ing verse)

Me and my boy are mad on dancin',
Never get goin'.
All we can do is walk to music
To-in' and fro-in'.
Night after night we practise hard
One-step, two-step, the lot.
All we can do is walk to music.
Goodness we do get hot.

Joyce shakes Irv's hand. Wipes her own down her skirt.
And pulls down stays on both sides.
Samba rhythm and Paddy advances.
Joyce with eyes shut, goes towards him in rhythm.
He again by-passes her for Beryl. Irv tries to swing

Palais Dancers

Music by Richard Addinsell

Originally performed by Joyce. Grenfell, Beryl Kaye, Paddy Stone and Irving Davies.

Boys in Teddy boy costumes. Mime of boredom, vanity and finally off to the pub.
Beryl enters. Goes back for Joyce. Joyce enters and shakes Irv's hand

> Me and my friend are mad on dancin',
> Me and my friend are.
> Me and my friend are quite ambitious,
> We'd like to go far.
> We've got dresses with sequins on,
> And layers and layers of lace.
> We go to the Palais once a week
> And keep up a *terrible* pace.

Joyce thinks Paddy is advancing to ask her but he by-passes her. She turns back and shakes Irv's hand

> Me and my friend began our dancin'
> At the same minute.
> Freda, my friend, is better at it,
> She puts more in it.
> We've got fellers who dance with us,

Joyce round. She stands firm. He manages two swings and then she goes right round, very injured and rubbing her shoulder. She pulls up her brassière. Rhythm change

> With a one and a two and a three and a four
> We can beat out a beat that is hot and sweet.
> With a two and a three and a four and a five
> Jingle, tingle, jingle and jive.
> One — two — three — four —

Irv joins her and they dance

> Me and my boy are mad on dancin',
> How am I doin'?
> Me and my boy are near a crisis,
> I can feel it brewin'.
> Though we struggle we don't progress:
> The reason is clear to see.
> He'd be all right if he was solo,
> His handicap is me.

Irv has joined Beryl and Paddy, and all three dance off. Joyce waves sadly

JOYCE GRENFELL REQUESTS THE PLEASURE, 1954

Mrs Mendlicote

In her fine, high, red brick house in Pont Street
At home Mrs Mendlicote waits.
For this is one of her famous Thursdays.
'At Home at Nine', the invitation states.

Tall Mrs Mendlicote stands by the fireplace.
(Where is her husband the world would know?)
Tall Mrs Mendlicote, alone and smiling,
Banked by hydrangeas and carnations' glow.

Candles are flickering in the candelabra,
People come drifting in, in ones, and twos, and threes.
'How enchanting . . . Lady Mary Waring . . .
Colonel Miller and dear Sir Godfrey Pease.'
(Where is her husband?
Where is her husband?)
'Canon Wardlow . . . Charlotte dear . . . and Mrs Lees.'

Pagliacci's heart was broken,
Mrs Mendlicote thought, and smiled,
Pagliacci's heart was broken,
Mine's still beating
Though its beating's rather wild.
He is gone, and gone forever,
'Please forgive me and forget.'

He is gone, and gone forever . . .
Mrs Mendlicote cannot quite
Realise it yet.

In her fine, high, red brick house in Pont Street
'At Home at Nine' the invitation states,
For this is one of her famous Thursdays.
Alone, at home, Mrs Mendlicote waits.

JOYCE GRENFELL REQUESTS THE PLEASURE, 1954

Young Musician, before Her First London Recital

This is the day of my piano recital — it's my first London recital — in a few minutes time I shall leave this nice, warm, safe, little artists' room and then I'll go down a few steps and up a few steps and out on to the platform. There's an old caretaker man who's going to tell me when.

I must be mad.

I don't remember a single word of anything I'm supposed to be playing. How does the Haydn begin? I mean just how does it . . .

Now, stop it. I got the whole thing sorted out in bed this morning. It's not in the *least* important. It's all going to be the same in a thousand year's time. It's not in the least important. But I wonder what all this agony is about? I mean *who is* going to enjoy it?

Mr Chilston will be suffering for me.

Except I suppose he must be used to pupils' recitals by now? But Mother will be suffering.

So will Daddy.

So will Aunt Helen.

And Miss Fortescue.

And *all* my friends.

So will Sam . . .

Oh, I don't suppose he'll come. Well, I suppose he might. He did put it in his little book. Only I don't think he ever looks at his little book. So I don't suppose he'll come.

Oh! How *does* the Haydn begin?

I mean just how . . .

Now, *stop* it. You know it absolutely backwards, so be quiet.

I wonder why people give recitals?

Because they want to I expect.

I must say I quite enjoyed doing the programme last week at the Music Club. But, of course, that was in the country. It's here in London that it's so idiotic. There are far too many recitals in London. Night after night people go all through this in this very hall. I should think there must be layers and layers of agony soaked into the walls by now.

And it's not as if anyone even wants to hear me play — yet. Or perhaps even ever. Only I suppose the thing you feel is that you might be able to *make* some-one listen one day. And you've got to start sometime.

I must say I did rather like seeing the posters. I saw one right up in Holborn. I wasn't in the least expecting it. I was just waiting for a bus and there was a woman standing next to me and I couldn't resist saying to Her: 'That's me.'

And she said: 'Oh, is it.'

The bus didn't come for *ages*.

I do hope my hair isn't going to come down.

Oh, I know, I must *not* forget to smile at the end of the first group. I *needn't* smile when I first go on. Mr Chilston said I needn't. Well, I couldn't anyway. But I must not forget to smile at the end of the first group.

I wonder if Myra Hess or Clifford Curzon ever feel like this?

I wish I was a singer.

I wish the whole thing was over and I was safely in bed and I needn't think about the piano for at least a week. Well, anyway not for two days. Well, not till tomorrow . . .

Oh, I remember the Haydn!

Oh, how silly. All that fuss. It's absolutely idiotic.

Wouldn't it be awful if someone came in here now and said I couldn't give the recital?

Oh —

Is it time?

Yes, I'm ready . . .

I'm quite ready . . .

JOYCE GRENFELL REQUESTS THE PLEASURE, 1954

Ethel

Music by Richard Addinsell

Music has sometimes been a stimulant when I was looking for ideas. I am loath to admit this because I thought that Viola Tunnard's tuition had taught me to listen so that I actually heard what was being played. But not. always. I went to a violin and piano recital of sonatas and thought I was paying attention to Brahms, when into my head crept the idea for a song about a quiet girl called Ethel whose character changed when she got to a football match. This was soon followed by the complete first verse. Going home in a taxi I wrote it out and never altered it. Thanks be to Brahms.

I don't understand Ethel.
I don't, I don't really.
She's one of my very best friends,
Just about the best, nearly.
She's an awfully nice girl, Ethel is,
Dainty and refined,
I mean she'd never do or say
Anything unkind.
But get her inside of a stadium
And she seems to go out of her mind.

'KILL HIM!' she yells, 'KNOCK HIS BLOCK
    OFF!'
At ice hockey or football or what.
'KILL 'EM!' she yells, turning purple,
'KILL THE PERISHING LOT!'
'SH-SH!' I say, *ETHEL!*'
'SH-SH!' and I die of shame.
'KILL HIM AND BASH HIS TEETH IN HIS
    FACE!'
She says,
And she calls him a dirty name.

> I don't understand Ethel,
> I don't I don't truly.
> She is always gentle and sweet,
> Never a bit unruly.
> She's an awfully shy girl, Ethel is,
> Wouldn't say boo to a goose.
> You wouldn't think she ever could
> Suddenly break loose.
> But get her inside of a stadium
> And her face turns a terrible puce.

'THROW HIM OUT OF THE WINDER!' she
    yells, 'AND WIPE HIM OUT!'
And her eyes go a terrible red,
'SWIPE 'EM!' she says, looking cheerful,
'SWIPE 'EM UNTIL THEY'RE DEAD!'
'SH-SH!' I say, *ETHEL!*'
'SH-SH!' and I nearly die.
'SWIPE HIM AND GRIND HIS FACE IN THE
    MUD!'
She says,
'AND PUT YOUR THUMB IN HIS EYE!'

I don't understand Ethel,
I don't I don't, really.
She's one of my very best friends,
Just about the best, nearly.
She's an awfully quiet girl, Ethel is,
That's why I never see
What makes her carry on like that,
Noisy as can be.
Then last Saturday down at the Stadium
Well — it suddenly happened to me.

'BREAK HIS SILLY NECK!' I yells, 'IRON
    HIM OUT!'
Well Ethel was startled at that.
'IRON HIM!' I says, feeling lovely,
'IRON HIM UNTIL HE'S FLAT!'
'OOH,' I says, *ETHEL!*'
'OOH,' and I did feel queer.
Then she grinned, and we both of us gave a
    yell,
'BITE A BIT OUT OF HIS EAR!'

JOYCE GRENFELL REQUESTS THE PLEASURE, 1954

Songs of Many Lands

Greetings to you all, fellow Culture Circle Members.

It is my privilege as a Founder Member of the Song Seekers Guild of America to bring you this evening some of the blooms I have gathered in Gardens of Song all the world over. I have tripped in many lands and among many lovely peoples, and nary a voyage has passed that I did not cull a garland or melody Where E'er I walked!

We of the Song Seekers Guild feel we are all each other's neighbour. And as we sing each other's songs so we look over into each other's backyard.

For a Song is a Hand Shake.

Isn't that a lovely Thought?

Here is a song from the Balkans that will do fitting well to ope our programme.

Some say that Marika's song has political implications. Some hold that it is an outcry against religious intoleration. Marika is headstrong. She stamps her foot at the least hint of criticism. If you listen you will hear the stamp of Marika's foot in the music.

> O Marika, ika, ika,
> Why do you smile at the soldiers?
> O Marika, ika, ika,
> Do you enjoy their company?

It is so dark in the forest, Marika,
Why do you smile at the soldiers?

And Marika replies:

I smile at the soldiers,
Because they are jolly fellows.
I smile at the soldiers to make the
    world go round.
I smile at the soldiers
Because it is Tuesday.

It is very interesting that Marika chooses Tuesday, because Tuesday is without any particular significance or peculiarity.

Let us move backwards down the years toward earlier days on the Isle of Phlaxos in the Azure Seas of the South. On the Isle of Phlaxos the women still make their famous lead cakes — so called because they are unleavened and lie heavy, and still wear the famous lace hood that dates from Crusader days.

This song is an invocation to a Cow. The music is a little complex so I will speak the lyric for you first.

In the small house of yesteryear
Dwells the wicked cow.
Why do you taunt me, O wicked cow?
Here is a silver bell for your horn,
Here is a straw hat for your ears,
Here is an egg for you,
And here is a wild boar to talk to you.
Now, will you give me milk?

(*To the accompanist*) Thank you.
(*He shakes his head*) But I gave you the music. It is

for the nose flute.

Well, there we are.

Now let us hie ourselves to the Low Countries whence cometh a merry song. There is a little play on words there. Hie and Low! Oh dear.

Our song tells the story of Pieter, a rich farmer who has a pig, a rick of straw, and a fine new pair of boots. He sallies forth into the market place to revel. But, alas, it is raining. He is woebegone. But see . . . Here comes Jansie, dancing down the street in her fur hat. He sings to Jansie:

> Good Morning, Jansie, ha ha ha,
> You are a fat girl, ho ho ho.
> Good morning Jansie, ha ha ha,
> I laugh to see you, ho ho ho!

I think it does us all good to laugh.

Finally from Central Europe comes this unusual and beautiful lullaby. Cecil Sharpe House of London had a version of this lullaby and they say it comes from the beautiful County of Lancashire. But after many years of research I hold the Central European version is the older and the more beautiful.

Picture now the mother, tired from her long day on the mountainside tending her goats. She has seen the sun rise, she has seen the sun set. All day her babe has been slung in a dried goat's skin across her back as she has climbed the mountain calling after her goats, for they roam far and wide. Goats do roam and it is very tiring calling after them. Now she is home in her little rude hut, builded of mud and goat skin, and the little one is in its rocking bed or cradle by the embers glow. The mother kicks the rocking bed or cradle to keep it in motion as she sings:

Sleep babeling, sleep, sleep,
Sleep babeling sleep.
Sleep babeling, sleep, sleep
Sleep babeling, sleep
Or thy mother will clout thee.

The version I use comes from the Urk Mountains of Central Europe, and I will sing it for you in the original Urk, 'Sloop Boobeling Sloop'.

Scholars have been puzzled by the significance of the clap at the end of the song, for surely it must wake the babe should he have dozed off? Still, it is traditional.

JOYCE GRENFELL REQUESTS THE PLEASURE, 1954

Ordinary Morning

Music by Richard Addinsell

It felt like an ordinary morning,
It began in an ordinary way,
And then without warning
Ordinary morning
Became extraordinary day

Hadn't the slightest sort of inkling —
No one said love was on its way —
And then within a twinkling,
Without the smallest inkling,
It became an extraordinary day.

For there you were
And the whole world stood still.
There you were
I loved you then and I always will.

At first, an ordinary morning,
Began in an ordinary way,
And then my heart was beating,
At this ordinary meeting

And we both knew
This was not an ordinary day.

It's Almost Tomorrow

Music by Richard Addinsell

It's almost tomorrow,
No longer today,
An hour that is timeless,
The right time to say
A sentimental goodbye to you,
No sorrow, tomorrow's in view.
It's almost tomorrow
And soon we must part,
Another new morning,
Another new start,
But now it's time to go on our way
And dream of tomorrow today.

Go on your way, on your way, on your way . . .

finale of JOYCE GRENFELL REQUESTS THE PLEASURE, 1954

The Whizzer

Music by Richard Addinsell

Originally performed by Elsie and Doris Waters and Sally Steward

Two ladies, probably members of the local
W.I., wearing Carnival Caps with mottoes,
but otherwise very *sensibly dressed.*

We shouldn't of gone on the Whizzer
We was lovely before we come out.
We wasn't delighted
Or over-excited,
Just glad to be gadding about.
'Have a bash,' said the Barker, 'You'll *love* it,
    I know,
It's ever so restful and nice.'
But we shouldn't of gone on the Whizzer at all,
Not on top of that floss
And that ice.

Win's not fond of Fair Grounds,
Fan is just the same.
But our neighbour, Connie Carter,
'Mad''s her middle name.
Mad she is for swing boats,
Mad for rides that dip,
Mad for roundabouts and dodg'ems,

Dotty for the Whip.
Then she sees this Whizzer,
'Come on, girls, let's go.'
So we climbs aboard the Whizzer.
How was we to know?
First it turned quite gently,
Pleasant as can be,
Then it worked itself up wicked
Turning speedily . . .
Faster, faster, faster . . .
Turning like a top . . .
Faster . . faster . . faster . . faster . . .
Wouldn't never stop.

Win and me was clinging,
Con was laughing, gay.
Then before our very faces
Con was whizzed away!
Whizzed above the housetops
Whizzed right out of sight,
Whizzed entirely from the picture
Whizzed into the night.

How to break the tidings?
Tell her family?
Connie whirled off of a Whizzer
To Eternity.

We shouldn't of gone on the Whizzer,
We only come here for some fun;
But it stood there so gay,
Only sixpence to pay,
And its music inside had begun.
We ought to of stuck to the Hoop-la —
Although every hoop was a loss —

But we shouldn't of gone on the Whizzer at all
Not on top of that ice
And that floss.

(Enter bearer of good tidings and whispers)

Con Carter's come down in a hayfield
A mile to the west of the town.
Oh, we're very relieved
For we never believed
That once up, Con would ever come down.
That's a merciful end to the story,
The story of Con, Fan and me.
But we shouldn't of gone on the Whizzer at all
Not on top of what we had for tea.

PAY THE PIPER, 1954

Career Girl

Music of Richard Addinsell

Originally performed by Elisabeth Welch

I am a Career Girl,
Sought after — Important — a Success.
I am a Career Girl
With her eye full of purpose
And a blazing eagerness
For Conferences — Meetings — and Interviews,
For Taking decisions and signing the Deal.
No time to sit and wonder,
No time to see my friends,
I work and work and never play,
My day never ends.
No one ever sees me without an appointment,
I'm Important — Successful — Complete.
But then,
When the telephone rings
And it's him,
And he calls —
Down fall the walls!

I grab a cab and drop what I am doing,
I cancel all appointments for the day.

I jam my hat on my head and I get going,
I'm glad I'm doing what I'm doing,
All the way.
I shut my eyes to any obligation,
I leave my office spinning like a top.
I sing a song as I go in mad elation,
I'm glad I'm doing what I'm doing,
I can't stop.
'Think of your career, my girl,
You've no time to spare.
You had better think twice.'
But I'm deaf to advice,
I don't care, I don't care, I don't care.
I grab a cab and shut my mind to duty,
I grab a cab and hurry anywhere
And when I arrive,
Only partially alive,
He's not there.

Now, no man can do that to a girl,
Not too often, that is,
If he's worth thinking of.
I return to my office
And take up the thread
And put out all thoughts of love from my head.
But then,
When the telephone rings
And it's him,
And he calls,
Down fall the walls!

I grab a cab and drop what I am doing,
I cancel all appointments for the day,
I double down the hall in a hurry.
Goodbye to worry, I must hurry

On my way.
I shut my eyes to any obligation,
I leave my office spinning like a top,
I sing a song as I go in mad elation,
I'm glad I'm doing what I'm doing,
I can't stop.
'Think of your career my girl,
You've no time to spare,
You had better think twice.'
But I am deaf to advice,
I don't care, I don't care, I don't care,
I grab a cab and fling myself inside it,
The driver drives as if he was insane.
I get to the door
Hardly breathing any more —
Not again!

Now, no man can do that to a girl,
Not *too* often that is.
Last week he called me one fine day
And I got my secretary to say,
'She's just about leaving,
She's going away,
Yes, she's leaving right now,
She's leaving today, at two.'
And what does he do?

He grabs a cab and drops what he is doing,
He cancels all appointments for the day.
His secretary gasps at what he's doing,
He must get going, must get going
On his way.
He can't believe this horrible sensation,
He watches every light as it turns red,
He shouts aloud in sheer exasperation.

He's not enjoying what he's doing,
I'm afraid!
What a fool I've been, he thinks.
He is in a state!
He is terribly low and the traffic is slow,
Not too late? Not too late? Not too late?
He grabs a cab and tells the man to race it,
He grabs a cab to find me anywhere.
And when he alights
And he runs up seven flights —
I'm there.

PAY THE PIPER, 1954

II
FOR SOLO
PROGRAMMES

**HENCEFORTH JOYCE GRENFELL
ACTED ON STAGE OR RADIO ONLY AS
A SOLO PERFORMER WITH
WILLIAM BLEZARD
AS HER ACCOMPANIST.**

Friend to Tea

At last — at last. The *Great* Day! Lovely to see you. Now, we're just going to relax and enjoy ourselves. I'm mad about your hat. But *mad*.

Now, where will you sit? Not too near the fire? Quite comfy? Well, forgive me if I just go and see if I remembered to turn off my iron. No, I'd *quite* finished — it's only a shirt — we're going somewhere *rather* grand tonight and one must look tidy. I'll put the kettle on and we'll have some tea. But do go on talking to me because I can still hear you because my kitchen is so near.

Have you seen Gordon lately? He's taken off his beard. I was so glad to see him again. Would you like some toast? Cake? Are you sure? Bicky then? Oh, you must have something. You're absolutely right. It's madness to eat.

There. Tell me everything — oh, that light's in your eyes. Oh, I'm so sorry, did I kick you? I can't bear a bright light in my eyes. I think it's so restless. I simply can't think with a bright light in my eyes.

Now — let's just relax. I want to hear everything. How is the family? And how is poor Ethel — I was rather worried when I heard she was tap-dancing again.

Oh, a cigarette — sit still — sit still — I'm such a bad hostess. I don't smoke myself and I never can remember to — isn't it a pretty box. Made by a Zulu.

When did you first suspect Robert? Ash tray?

And what did he say? And what did you say? Well done — I bet that stopped him.

Go on (I'm just going to close the window, we're in a complete draught and I think it's so restless sitting in a draught). Go on. He's so insensitive — just like his mother — m'm.

(I'm just going to put a piece of wood on the fire. It's rather cold in here.) Did you know you're not supposed to touch a person's fire unless you've known them for seven years? My dear, you're supposed to just sit there and let the fire go out and everybody freeze to death. It's the sort of idiotic old wives' tale that makes me *so* cross. But I'm not going to be cross while you're here. You know you have the most marvellous effect on me — I feel quite, quite different — completely relaxed and peaceful.

D'you know, at this moment there's a picture above your head that is so crooked I simply must just put it straight. I think there's nothing so restless as a crooked picture. I'll just see if our kettle is ready? What tea do you like — Indian or China? I don't mind in the least. No, you say. Go on. All right, then we'll have both. No, the kettle isn't ready yet.

Have you seen Mabel lately?

No, I haven't, but she lent me the most extraordinary book. No, it's not like that — it's — it must be in my bedroom — I think you'd love it, it's called *Flesh*.

I tell you what you would love.

I've got the most exciting new record of Spanish flameco singing. It's *so* exciting — I mean it is Spain — the heat and the dust and the rhythms. You simply can't sit still.

There, I can hear the kettle's ready. Now, you haven't told me anything yet.

Now, begin at the beginning.

Oh, I must tell you I've learnt to make a soufflé. My dear, it's easy. The whole secret is the whipping — I mean it's . . .

Do you smell something funny?

I know I turned the iron off — you saw me do it. D'you know, I didn't.

1957

Committee

*The ladies are assembled in Mrs Hailestone's
front room somewhere north of Birmingham.
The telly is full on. It is time to start the
meeting.*

Well, let's get down to business, shall we?

Would you be so good as to turn off your telly,
please, Mrs Hailestone? Thank you. That's better. It's
very good of you to let us use your front room. I
think we're all assembled. Mrs Brill, Miss Culch, Mrs
Pell, Mrs Hailestone, May and me. All right then, May,
let's have the minutes of the last meeting.

Oh, May. You're supposed to have them in that
little book I gave you. I told you last time. You're
supposed to write down everything we do and say
and then read it out at the next meeting, and I sign it.

I know we all know what we said and did, dear,
but you have to write it down. That's what minutes
are for.

Don't cry, May, dear. Let's get on with the next
item on the agenda. Apologies for Absence. You read

136

out the excuses. Oh, May. Well, you must try and remember to bring your glasses next time. All right, I'll read them. Give them here. Cheer up.

Mrs Slope is very sorry she's caught up. Can't come.

Miss Heddle's got her mother again. Can't come.

Lady Widmore sent a telegram 'ALAS CANNOT BE WITH YOU DEVASTATED'. Can't come.

Well then. As you all know, this is *another* special meeting of the Ladies' Choral to talk about the forthcoming Festival and County Choral Competition. We know the date and we know the set song. Yes we do, May. It's in two parts for ladies' voices in E flat, 'My Bosom is a Nest'.

But of course what we are really here for tonight is this very important question of voices in the choir. Now, we don't want any unpleasantness. Friendly is what we are, and friendly is how we are going to go on. But it's no good beating about the bush, we all know there is *one* voice among the altos that did not ought to be there. And I think we all know to what I am referring.

Now, don't think that I don't like Mrs Codlin, because I do. Yes, she *is* a very nice woman. Look at how nice she is with her little car — giving us all lifts here and there. And she's a lovely lender — lends you her books, and her knitting patterns, recipes, anything. Lovely. Yes, she is a regular churchgoer *and* a most generous donator to the fund. But she just has this one fault: she does not blend.

May, dear, would you be so kind as to slip out and see if I left the lamp turned off on my bike? I don't want to waste the battery, and I can't remember if I did it. Thank you, May.

Ladies, I didn't like to say anything in front of May, but I must remind you that Mrs Codlin's voice is worse than what ever May's was, and you know what happened the last time we let May sing in the competition. We were disqualified. So you see it is very important and very serious.

Oh thank you, May, dear. Had I? I am a big silly, aren't I?

You see, it isn't as if Mrs Codlin had a voice you could ignore. I mean you can't drown her out. They can hear her all down the road, over the sopranos; yes, over your piano, Mrs Pell, over everything. You know, I was stood next to her at practice last week when we did 'The Wild Brown Bee is my Lover'. When we'd finished I said to her very tactfully, thinking she might like to take the hint, I said: 'I wonder who it is stands out so among the altos?' and she said she hadn't noticed. Hadn't noticed! Mrs Brill was on her other side and she said to me afterwards, didn't you, Mrs Brill? she said the vibrations were so considerable they made her chest hum.

No, I know she doesn't do it on purpose, May.

No, of course she didn't ought to have been let in in the first place. It's ridiculous. It makes a nonsense of music. But the thing is, it was her idea, wasn't it? She founded the choir.

Do you think if anyone was to ask her very nicely not to sing it might stop her? I mean we could let her come and just stand there. Yes, Mrs Hailestone, she does *look* like a singer, I'll give her that. That's the annoying part.

Would anybody like to ask her? Well, has anybody got any suggestions?

No, May, not anonymous letters. They aren't very nice.

I wonder . . . May, one of your jobs as secretary is watching the handbags and the coats at competitions, isn't it? I mean you have to stay in the cloakroom all during the competitions, don't you? I thought so. Look, May; now don't think we don't appreciate you as a secretary — we do, dear, don't we ladies? — But would you like to resign? Just say yes now, and I'll explain it all later.

Well, we accept your resignation, and I would like to propose that we appoint Mrs Codlin secretary and handbag-watcher for the next competition. Anybody second that? Thank you, Mrs Hailestone. Any against? Then that's passed unanimously. Lovely. Oh, I know it's not in order, Mrs Pell, but we haven't any minutes to prove it. May didn't have a pencil, did you, May?

Well, I think it's a very happy solution. We get rid of her and keep her at one and the same time.

What did you say, May? Can *you* sing if Mrs Codlin doesn't?

Oh, May, you've put us right back to square one.

1957

Wibberly

ANNOUNCER: Good evening. This evening we are taking television viewers to another historic house in our series of Historic British Houses and this evening we are to visit ... Wibberly ... the ancient castle home of the Earls of Wibberly since the thirteenth century. And here to greet us is our hostess, Lady Wibberly.

LADY WIBBERLY: Is it me now? Yes, I am ready. Which camera did we say I was to look at? This one. Right. Shall I begin? Right.

GOOD EVENING AND A VERY WARM WEL-COME TO OUR BELOVED OLD WIBBER — I needn't do it quite so loud? Oh, I see. I mustn't do it quite so loud.

Well, here we are in the entrance hall which is a Victorian addition to the castle proper and here as you see we have our very remarkable stained-glass dome which was put up by my husband's grandfather as a surprise for his wife. And in here, too, we have our eight over life-size white marble statues of the Greek gods, each one ready and waiting on his plinth ... as indeed am I ... to welcome you *all* to our beloved old Wibberly.

Well, now this is Apollo — whom I expect you know? And this one is ... Well, I know this one is

140

Apollo and somewhere we do have Mercury with his little feathered hat. Never mind.

When I was a girl I used to come and stay at Wibberly — before I married Lord Wibberly — and one was always so amused because they used the statues as a sort of extra coat room and one would come in and find the statues festooned in all manner of coats and capes and rain coats and macintoshes! . . . One was always so entertained. And not only was it a good place to put the coats, but it was also a very clever place to dry them off because we have in here — somewhere — a grating through which comes hot air and I know of nothing pleasanter on a cold winter's day than to come in here and stand over the grating.

Now let us go into the castle proper and here we are in the Long Gallery with its Rembrandts, its Vermeers, Constables, Van Dykes, Van Goghs . . . The walls are panelled in . . . some dark wood . . . but I think to me the main interest in here lies in the collection of watercolour sketches painted by beloved old mother-in-law, Ethel, Lady Wibberly at the advanced age of eighty-four. Over night, as it were, she fell in love with watercolour paints and her forte was hollyhocks and we have in here thirty-seven studies of hollyhocks. I think you may notice them hanging among our other lovely treasures.

The plaster work in here is sixteenth century and the fluorescent strip-lighting is rather more recent.

Now, let us go in to the Elizabethan Banqueting Hall.

(Do I go first or does the camera? I go first. It's so clever isn't it? I'm afraid I don't understand television. We haven't got a set I'm afraid. We can't afford it.)

Here we are in the Elizabethan Banqueting Hall, with its Musicians' Gallery, empty, alas, now except for some potted plants. We do not dine in here any more. It is four hundred yards from the kitchen — and only one maid — one never had a hot meal . . . But we all come in here on wet days and have such fun playing ping-pong.

Up there is rather a charming gargoyle one is very devoted to. He is really a drain! And at first one wondered what a drain was doing indoors! But we didn't have to worry because he doesn't work.

Over there in the glass case is one of our great treasures and that is Oliver Cromwell's button. It's rather a tiny button, I'm afraid — we don't really know quite where it — but it *is* Oliver Cromwell's very own button. Is the camera on me or on the button? Oh, it's on the button. It's very nice not to have it on me for a moment. Oh, it's on me again now. Back again.

Finally I want you to see our greatest Wibberly treasure of all, and that is Glyndowena's Tower with its echo chamber. It has rather a charming little legend. Glyndowena was married to the first Lord Wibberly in the thirteenth century — we were only Barons then — and he was away a very great deal — travelling — and she was very lonely, so she built this Tower with its Echo Chamber that she might go into it, talk to herself and be answered by the echo. It's very moving, isn't it? One sees her alone there with her echo . . .

I would love you to hear the echo. We are so proud of it. It's rather exciting.

Hullo?

I didn't hear it, did you? Let's have another go. HULLO?

You know, sometimes when it is at all damp one doesn't . . .

ANNOUNCER: Owing to a breakdown in transmission we have had to leave Wibberly Castle.

1957

Shirley's Girl Friend 1

Fun Fair

The series of 'Shirl' scripts originated on radio at the end of the war, and I wrote a great many sketches for this South London girl in conversation with her friend, Shirl.

Shirl, I thought you wasn't never going to see me again the other night! It's a fact. Well, you know my boy Norm? You know, the one that drives the lorry with the big ears? Well, him. The other day it was Norm's Mum's birthday, so we all goes over to the Fun Fair for a bit of laugh, see. Four of us, Norm, Norm's Mum and Norm's Mum's lodger, Mr Pilchard, and me. Mr Pilchard is the one that went on *What's My Line* once and nobody never guessed him. He's an advert dropper. You know. Drops the adverts through your letter box and hands you one in the street you don't want as you go by. Dear old soul.

Well, we gets to this Fun Fair and Norm says that wild horses wouldn't get him on to any side-show that goes round and round.

Because he can't do with it, Shirl. He just turns green and you have to be very nice to him. Mr Pilchard says he don't mind coming down the Twisted Tower on a little mat but he draws the line at going on the Giant Wheel, but of course it is this Giant Wheel that Norm's Mum is so dead set on going on, see.

Funny her being set on anything so daring loike because she is more on the nervy side. I mean she don't like lighting the gas, and she can't come down a ladder once she's gone up it, and she always feels funny after fish. But this Giant Wheel! She's mad for it.

You know the Giant Wheel, don't you Shirl? It's that big huge wheel you see sticking out of the top of Fun Fair Grounds before you get there. It's got like little seats hanging off of it and when the wheel turns you might think the little seats is going to turn over too, but they never. They just go on hanging down like.

It's scientific.

Well, Norm's Mum says it's *her* birthday and she is going to go on the Giant Wheel willy or nilly. So I says, 'Have a heart, Mum,' and she says she hasn't got one. Only a swinging brick. So I can't let her go alone, can I? So I tells Norm and Mr Pilchard to go and have a nice sit and wait for us to come looming up over the horizon. Norm's Mum says to me, 'You are going to love it. It's like you got wings on.' 'Well,' I says, 'we all got to go in the end if your name is on it.'

We get to the little platform where you get on from and the attendant says, room for one here, so Norm's Mum goes in the seat with a sailor and I got to share with a young Teddy Boy feller with all his hair cut off short.

I says, 'Good evening.'

And he says, 'Hullo.'

And I says, 'Nice weather for the time of year.'

And he never looks at me but just says, 'So what?'

'Well,' I says, to try and cheer him up, 'It's better than a slap in the face with an old boot.' But he don't laugh.

Well, we fastens ourselves into our seats and the engine starts going very slowly and we start to go up and up, and when we get to the top of the circle like everybody gives a little scream because it feels like you are going to turn over, but you don't and it's nice to have a little scream. I always like a nice little scream when it's for pleasure.

Well, we done the circle two or three times and had our little screams, and then all of a sudden, when me and this Teddy Boy feller are right up at the top, the wheel stops!

Gone wrong, see.

We wait a minute and nothing happens only silence, so I calls down to Norm's Mum in her seat below ours, 'Are you all right?'

And she says, 'What?'

And I says, 'Are you all right?'

And she says, 'I'm all right, ta, I got a sailor with his arm round me waist,' and she laughs. She's always been one for sailors ever since she can remember.

I don't get much out of my Teddy Boy feller. He just sits there brewing. I might as well have been invisible. After a minute I says to him, 'We're stuck up here, you know?'

And he says, 'So what?'

'Well,' I says, 'thanks for the chat. Mind you don't wear yourself out talking. What you come to the Fun Fair for?'

And he says, 'For the thrill.'

'Oh,' I says, 'Did you get it?'

145

He says, 'No.'

So I try singing to myself. I done 'We'll Gather Lilacs', and 'Life is Just a Bowl of Cherries', and 'Trees'. But he don't take no notice, so I touch his arm to see if he's dead and he says, 'I don't like it up here.'

So I says, 'No more do I but I'm looking on the bright side and enjoying the fresh air and all.'

I think to meself what's happened to Norm and Mr Pilchard? You'd of thought they'd of noticed we hadn't come down by now. There's a crowd collected and everyone is looking up, and by and by I recognise Norm by his ears so I give him a yell and he looks up and hollers at me, 'How'd you get up there?'

So I says, 'I got flew up on a broomstick,' and everybody laughs, and Norm says, 'You come down here,' he says, 'you don't half look silly stuck up there.' I says, 'Look Mr Clever,' I says, 'Why don't you go and mend what's wrong, you being a trained motor mechanic and all.'

He stands there for a minute, then I see him push his way through the crowd to where the engine is, and he talks to some of the men and takes his coat off and tampers with this and that, and after a minute the engine starts again and we come down!

Well, of course Norm is the hero of the hour and everybody sings 'For he's a Jolly Good Feller', and Norm turns red and says it wasn't nothing. It was only a bolting leech-kleet got devalved off of the swithin circuit, and he got it on again.

I says, 'Fancy knowing how to get a bolting leech-kleet back on to a devalved swithin circuit! You don't look like you could do it but you done it.' And he says, 'I never meant it when I said you looked silly stuck up there.' He says, 'You're all right,' and I says,

'So are you,' and he says, 'Shut up.'
  Oh, he is nice.

1957

Christmas Eve

Today with a list of jobs to be done
As long as my arm,
And too many people in too many places
    pushing,
Christmas has lost its charm.
What with neon signs blazing and dazing
As they changed,
And nothing left in the shops . . .
No wrapping paper, tags or scarlet string,
Not a *thing* left . . .
And the wear and tear
Of trying to get from A to B
And no time to spare for transit —
Oh, I lost sight of Christmas.
'Well, it's not for me anyway,' I said,
'It's for the children.'
And I waited, tapping my foot,
On an island in mid-traffic,
While the lights deliberately stuck

To prevent me or anybody else
Getting anywhere.
'Oh Lor',' I said,
'Look at that terrible pink, plastic duck
In a sailor's hat
Going by under a woman's arm.
What's that a manifestation of?
Thank heaven there are no more shopping days
    to Christmas.'

Christmas?
Oh, Christmas. I'd forgotten.
I looked along the busy city thoroughfare.
The holly colours in a hundred rear lamps
Made their small contribution.
Red buses rumbled by, loaded with individuals
And their packages and private plans for
    tomorrow.
A street band blew a carol.
The pink glow above the city
Hid the star,
But the street was bright with more than
    electricity
And through a crack in a man-made world
I caught a glimpse of the glory
And the good of Christmas.

1957

The Woman on the Bus

Music by Richard Addinsell

'If I had a wish,'
Said the woman on the bus,
'I know what I'd like to see.
I'd like a great big enormous gorgeous party
And the belle of the ball is me.
And I'd take a walk down a circular stair
In a rich red velvet gown.
There'd be a great big enormous gorgeous silence
As I come a-willowing down.
I'd get all the neighbours to come along,
The Queen and the Prince as well,
And all the film stars, the telly ones too,
And some newspaper fellers to tell us all about
    it.'
'If I had a wish,'
Said the woman on the bus,
'I know what I'd like to see . . .

"Oh, who is this fascinating lady fair,
A-coming down the marvellous marble stair
With a ruddy great tiara in her hair?"
And I'd say, "Turn it up, IT'S ME!" '

1957

All We Ask Is Kindness

Music by Richard Addinsell

Beyond the call of duty
Every wife must stand,
Lending strength and beauty
To the task in hand.
Working like a beaver
Always with a smile
Ready to take the rough and smooth
To go the extra mile.
But service needs rewarding,
Just some tiny sign,
Helps to make a woman feel
She is doing fine.

All we ask is kindness,
Just a hint of praise.
We'll make do with a word or two.
We don't need a blaze of glory,

We're not after flattery, don't need to be admired.
But it's not enough at the end of the day
When you've been wearing yourself away
To see him stand in the door and hear him say
'Coo — I'm tired.'

1957

Dear François

Music by Richard Addinsell

Out of the blue I write to you to say that all is well in
London still. I trust your wife is well? — You too? Do
write and tell me all your news. My daughter, Adrianne,
is seventeen today. I thought you'd like to know —
after so long — that all is well here.

> I wish you could see my daughter
> She's not in the least like me.
> She's small and dark and lightly made,
> Not in the least bit English, I'm afraid.
> I wish you could see my daughter
> She's amusing and she's kind.
> She's got a lively mind, like you.
> I'm very proud of her.
>
> There's no excuse for writing now,
> I thought I never would.

154

What's past is past
And both of us are happy now
And so the news is good.
Perhaps I'm wrong in writing
But the war's so far away —
Another world,
But I am grateful for the past today.

I wish you could know my daughter,
Oh, I'm prejudiced I agree,
But none the less she does impress
Everyone else and so it's not just me.
I felt I must talk about her,
But it's the middle of the night
And a foolish time to write.
I said I never would.

Dear François
Have no fear, I will not fail.
This letter will not reach you
That I swear.
I write you every year
But none of my letters
Ever catch the mail.

1959

Boat Train

'Boat Train' was a tear-jerker, based on an
incident I witnessed at Waterloo Station,
with this difference: the real-life mother
seeing off her grown-up son and his wife
and family to settle in a far country was
full of self-pity; the woman I wrote about
was so distressed at the parting that she
made light of it to spare her children.
Gallantry again. Of all human qualities I
find selfless courage the one I admire most.

My son and his family are sailing away
To start an adventure
Across the sea.
They've sold up their house,
Said goodbye to the neighbours,
So now all that's left is
Their goodbye to me.
I think they dread it,
Standing here in the station,
They dread I'll be soppy

156

When I say goodbye.
It's a grey sort of morning.
I wish they would go now,
Not much to say now
Except Cheeri-bye.

'Well, good riddance I say!
I'm glad to be rid of you —
Oh, I'll be all right,
Don't you worry about me.
It's a good job you're going,
I'm sick of the sight of you!
Oh, I'll be all right.
Just think I'll be free,
Just think of the Whist Drives that I can attend!
The programmes on TV I'll be able to *choose*!
Just think of the leisure,
Just think of the pleasure I'll have on my own.
Why, there's no time to lose!

No more phoning and saying:
'Mum, can you come over?'
'Mum, can you take Bill to the dentist, and then
Mum, can you fetch Jean and the twins from their
    dancing?'
'Mum, can you come over?
We've been asked out this evening.'
Mum, could you and would you
Again and again.

So good riddance I say
It's high time I got started.
There's so much to do
I'll start now — you'll see.
It's a good job you're going,

You won't see me gallivanting!
Oh, I'll be all right,
Don't you worry about me!

Look! There, the guard's getting ready,
Jump in, loves . . . no tears.
Mind you write to me often,
Take care now, my dears.
Mind you write to me often,
Have a good time . . . don't cry . . .
Goodbye, my dear darlings,
Goodbye . . .
Goodbye . . .

1959

Life Story

The character is the wife of a musician: she is of middle European origin, with an accent.

So, you are going to write a book about my husband! And I would like to help you all I can. You know, of course, of his world-wide fame as a pianist, but perhaps you do not know that he was also quite a family man.

A book about my husband! I think he would laugh if he could know. He did not take himself so serious. Oh no; no, no.

Yes, I think you could say he was — what is your word? — gregarious. He was always very popular from the start. I think I would say he had what I would call a hospitable heart.

We were both students when we met and we got married. I was in music then. Singer — with piano as second study; but you cannot have two full-time musicians in one family when there are the children. There are tourings and rehearsals and concerts and so I was the one to stay home and sing the lullaby and I gave the children their first lessons on the piano. Yes, I still play a little bit. Nothing much — yes, I still sing sometimes, for myself. But nothing very much.

No, I never went out to Australia. My husband is going many times. Clara Ross? You mean the Australian singer? Yes, she was a friend for my husband and when she is in England she is coming to our house and I am also hearing her in concert and opera etc, etc. What a voice! I think it is the most wonderful voice that there is. Marvellous.

No, I did not go to South Africa, either. So many places I am not going! My husband is making many tours there. Oh, you mean the South African writer, Marta Van der Velt? Yes, she was a friend for my husband and after he is making a long concert tour he is going to stay with her. She is having a most beautiful house and garden in a place called Natal, I think — and he would go there for a holiday and he would write me marvellous letters about the flowers and the beaches and the sun and, you know, now I sometimes feel I have been there and seen it all for myself.

I have got all his letters, safely put away — I think they will be very useful for the book.

I don't know what I would say was his favourite kind of music. He made many recitals and piano concerts with orchestra; but I think perhaps his most favourite was chamber music. He loved chamber music and he made many sonata recitals.

Yes, with Clothilde Neilson, the French violinist. Many recitals. And later with Olga Wellitsche, the cellist. Many tours, many, many tours.

You know when he was away my husband would write little tunes, such *homesick* tunes, for the children to play on the piano.

I think people do not know or understand the life

of a musician. It is not just the platform and the applause, it is the long journeys, and time changes and different food and hotels and travelling. A musician's life is not just all skittles and beer.

Oh yes, he is going to America. He loved America. He said the best audiences in the world for music is in America because they are all Europeans living in America!

And to Hollywood. He was many, many times in Hollywood in the days when Hollywood *was* Hollywood.

Shirley Brewster? You mean the comedienne? She is our family favourite. We never miss one of her pictures. She is so funny . . .!

I did not know she was a friend for my husband. He had very good taste.

Now — you are going to write this book about my husband and I am going to help you all I can. There is just one thing I would ask that you should know and remember. My husband always — he always came home to *me*.

1959

Counter-Wise

Brooklyn accent

Can I help you, Madam?

Oh, Celeste! I thought you were a real customer. I was going to try my Sales Psychology on you. How's the Beauty Salon business doing upstairs?

Oh, I'm fine. Full of Sales Psychology up to here. You know: 'We've got it — you don't want it — but you're going to buy it' type stuff. We been having lectures, see. Our Mr Hirschman says to me: 'Miss Seidlitz, I want to further you. I want you should go learn to earn. Take a course in the Psychology of Selling.' So I had to go. Well, they was compulsive lectures, you gotter go willy or nilly. Still, it was interesting ... and in the firm's time, too. So ...

They got this lecturer ... middle-size college-graduate type feller. Black tweeds and loafers. Very casual. No ulcers ... and he says: 'Look, we're going to work this thing out together. We are in business to do business. Right? So selling is our sacred duty and we might as well be happy selling. Don't forget,' he

162

says, 'Pleasantness Pays Off. Come on now, let's see you girls smile.' So we all smile. All except Anna Polowski. You know Anna? She's got no ambition. She says from the bottom you got no place to fall off of from — but me, I got ambition so I smile and he says you got to practise that smile till it comes natural. You got to practise a sincere smile because Selling is a War and your Weapon is a Smile.

So I go home and practise on my old man and he says: 'You sick or som'pn? Don't do that ... you make me nervous.' So I move to the bathroom — our place is so small — and I work on developing my personality because what type goods you are selling, that type personality you got to develop. I mean, f'rinstance — if you are selling stationery or personalised lingerie, you got to be refined, but if you are in something robust like hardware, or like I am here in Notions, then you got to be robust. Don't stifle your natural ebulgence, let yourself go. Be the 'Hi-there-fellers-who's-for-the-steak-dinner-with-onions-type girl'.

Well, here I am in Notions, remembering that Selling is a War and my Weapon is a Smile and in comes a little smarty-pants type woman knows all the answers with a little smarty-pants type hat on. 'Pleasantness Pays Off,' I say to myself, so I smile and she says: 'I bet you don't have any of that new rug cleanser I seen on television last night. All you got to do is fluff it on and fluff it in and fluff it off.' So I says, very pleasant and sincere: 'I'm sorry but I was to my sister's last night and we didn't see no television. What is the name of the product you are desiring to obtain?' And she says: 'It's called *Fluffitoff!*'

Well, Celeste, I know this product and it's no good, so I say: 'Madam, if you have a rug you are fond of, do not let it get near this *Fluffitoff*. I mean, if it's only some old rug you don't give a damn about then, OK, OK, but if it is a good quality rug then I'm telling you, friend to friend, do not let it go near to *Fluffitoff*.' She looks at me like a dagger and she says: 'It may interest you to know that my husband happens to manufacture *Fluffitoff*.' So I say: 'Well, I'm sorry to hear it.' And she says: 'Why? What's wrong with *Fluffitoff*?'

I tell her it's got this ingredient in it is too fierce. Not only is it removing the stains off the rug already but it is also removing the rug pattern at one and the same time.

She says: 'This is terrible. We got a coast to coast campaign to launch this product with top quality advertising, etc. Are you sure about it?' 'Absolooly,' I says. 'My sister used it . . . and phifff no rug pattern.' 'Oh,' she says, 'I must go right down to my husband's office and call in the merchandise for a re-analysis. We got to stop it before it's too late. I want to thank you for being so honest and sincere. I want to thank you very much.' I says: 'Think nothing of it. Be my guest, it's a pleasure.'

Well, Mr Hirschman comes over and says to me: 'I can see you have really benefited from our lectures, Miss Seidlitz. Pleasantness sure Pays Off,' and I said: 'You are so right, Mr Hirschman.' And I felt good, you know, giving a helping hand along the way, and you know som'pn, Celeste, I have *just this minute* realised that the cleanser my sister used on her rug was called *Wipeitaway*: I think I'll move to Chicago. . .

1959

164

Simple Setting

Upper crust New Yorker

I think it's so exciting that you want to paint my portrait, Mr Hindhorst. Now, this is the little white room I told you about because I thought it might be the right setting for the picture. I've just finished decorating it and I'm crazy about it. You see, I've kept it deliberately stark — brutally white walls and absolutely basic — like a cell, because I want it to be a place of utter honesty where I can be absolutely myself. Very little furniture, you see, and only that piece of sculpture to focus your eye on.

Do you like it? It's a portrait bust of me in pig iron.

It's a Girder Loomb. Do you know his work? I think he is going to be very important. It's exciting isn't it. So relentless and so contemporary — utterly without compromise. And I think it's so interesting that he saw me as a series of ellipses. It seems to move in all directions, doesn't it? You know, sometimes I really rather wish I did look like that.

Oh, you think I *do*? Oh.

No, I don't mind a bit, I think it's wonderful. I think one ought to look of one's own period. It's just that people will tell you things. Oh, I don't know. Well, a man I knew once always said he saw me in a niche — he said I was pure Baroque and I belonged in a niche. But he was a little crazy at the time. To think he even wrote a sonnet about it, bless his heart. Such a darling person. Do you know his work? Ricki Bott. He's quite well known among new writers. He publishes in Italy. I think he's going to be *very* important.

Where are you going to sit? Are you bothered by these low sofas? It's the Japanese influence and I think they are amusing and you get an entirely different point of view of a party from lying down on one. No, do walk round and get the feel of the room. You want to get the feel of me? Thank you.

No, do smoke your pipe.

I don't know if you like to know about your sitters but I think it's so important to know what goes on behind the mask, don't you?

I'm a very simple person actually. I love everything that's simple and true. I love people. I love little people — like cab drivers, and little old ladies in the park. And homemade bread and shiny red apples, and children. I'm crazy about children because I think they have the secret of the whole thing — and they're so tender and so vulnerable and sensitive —

Patsy darling! Don't ever come bouncing into the room like that again, you nearly scared me out of my mind. Say how-do-you-do to Mr Hindhorst. This is my daughter Patsy, Mr Hindhorst. You think we look alike? Like sisters! Oh, what a divine thing to say. Thank you very much.

Patsy, if Mr Hindhorst thinks we look like sisters, it isn't very nice to tell him he's wrong. Yes, I know I

166

told you you must always be honest, but sometimes it isn't always — What did you want darling? Because I'm very busy. Talking to Mr Hindhorst. About lots of things. Shall we tell her? Mr Hindhorst very sweetly wants to paint my portrait. Because he thinks it's a good idea. Now, run along Patsy and get something to do. And close the door after you. All right — PLEASE close the door.

I'm so sorry, Mr Hindhorst, but I'm afraid she's at the questing stage and I do try to be available when she needs me. I think it's very important.

(*Coughs*) What kind of tobacco are you using, Mr Hindhorst? Leaves? You mean ordinary leaves off trees? How fascinating. I thought it was a little different. I expect it is economic. No, go ahead — I love it.

Do you want a little music on the phonograph while we talk? I've just discovered Palestrina and I'm in a daze. But maybe we ought to concentrate. Do you think it might be a good idea to paint me holding a book? I could wear something with a very full skirt, sort of casual. I could telephone and have something made at Balmain and they'd fly it over. They have my measurements. Might be fun, don't you think? Sort of grey velvet, like a Quaker. Do you really think I do? You're very sweet.

Patsy darling, I told you to go away.

Because I'm busy and it doesn't smell stinky in here. (*Cough*) Mr Hindhorst uses a very different kind of tobacco. I haven't asked him why. Patsy, I don't want to have to speak to you again. Now, go away and do something. And close the door, please. All right, you may get yourself some ice-cream from the freezer — And some cake.

Sometimes she's very like her father.

Mr Hindhorst, I was so fascinated about your portrait exhibition. You called it 'Twenty Seven Faces', didn't you? May I ask you a question? Was it a gimmick and is it symbolic of something or did all your twenty-seven sitters really each wear a black eye patch?

That's the way you saw them? How exciting.

You are so original.

And now I'm dying to ask you — How do you see *me*?

In a niche!

Well, you aren't the first, Mr Hindhorst.

With my face to the wall!

Oh . . .

1959

You Don't Need More than a Small, Bare Room

Music by Richard Addinsell

You don't need more than a small, bare room
Full of love, love, love.
Who needs more than a small, bare room
Where there's love, love, love?
Thoughts are company,
Peace is wealth,
You can't do better
Than a pocketful of health!
You don't need more than a small, bare room
Where there's love, love, love.

You don't need more than a small, bare room
Full of love, love, love.
(And a table and chair and a bed.)
Who needs more than a small, bare room
(With a rug on the floor, a radio, a television set,
A telephone, some books, oh, and a bathroom.)
Where there's love, love, love?

Thoughts are company,
Peace is wealth,
You can't do better
Than a pocketful of health!
You don't need more than a small, bare room
(With a fully-equipped kitchen off it, a garden full

Of flowers, a garage with a car in it and an attractive
Man with a private income)
And love, love, love.

1959

Golden Wedding

Music by Richard Addinsell

Oh my, I'm glad that's over, our Golden Wedding
   Day,
It's been a great occasion in every kind of way.
Our Golden Celebration, how could it come so
   soon?
T'was only yesterday we went on our
   honeymoon.
How nice to see the children and all the family,
Four generations gathered here — because of you
   and me!

We seem to have come into harbour, Herbert,
The sea is calm and clear,
There were hummocky times on the way, Herbert,
But anyhow, now we're here.
And I don't remember the storms too well,
My memory is so blest!
And if either of us ever wandered . . . a little . . .?
Neither of us confessed.
What's not spoken is soon forgotten,
It's wiser not to know.
I always think unburdening is a great mistake
And so
We seem to have come into harbour, Herbert,
The scenery is fair

And the hummocky times have vanished
  completely
And look! my love, we're there.

Oh my, I'm glad it's over, our Golden Wedding
  Feast,
It *is* a sort of milestone to say the very least.
I'm glad they've all gone home now, I'm sleepy now,
  aren't you?
So many lovely presents — what *are* we going to
  do?
What an important question: Will you for good or
  bad
Take Herbert for your husband? Yes. I did and I'm
  quite glad.

And now are you glad that you wed me, Herbert?
That we have come so far?
Herbert? Herbert, are you asleep?
Yes, of course you are.

1959

Telephone Call

Originally written for and performed by Bettina Welch in Sydney, Australia.

> Scene. Somewhere near Sydney, Australia.
> Marianne is about thirty. Until lately she
> worked in a shop in the city. She had just
> given her father his mid-day dinner. She
> comes in, calling over her shoulder.

Dad, go and settle yourself in your chair outside. I'll bring the tea as soon as the kettle's ready. Mind the step as you go. Well, you missed it yesterday. OK . . . OK . . . I'm not fussing.

Hullo — Ken?

It's me.

'Hullo Beautiful,' yourself.

Busy? Sorry to call you now but it's so hard to find a time when Dad's not near the phone.

He's out on the porch.

Oh, about the same. But it 's been a bad morning after a bad night. He couldn't sleep.

Look, Ken, I can't come out tonight.

Because I can't leave him.

Yeah . . . he's got the radio and he's got the dog and it's high time he got used to being left on his own — etc, etc. But I can't leave him tonight, because he gets the willies when he's left alone in the house and I

173

wouldn't have a minute's peace worrying ... you know ... imagining things and that.

Dear — I *do* want to come.

I know it's been going on like this for ages.

Ken — don't say that.

You don't wish it. You mustn't.

No, I don't — I couldn't.

He's my father.

Damn — he's yelling for me. Hang on.

(*Calls*) It hasn't boiled yet, Dad. What? Oh, all right, I'll be out in a minute to hear the play. You start listening.

He's got a play on the radio he wants me to listen to with him.

Yes, he can hear it if we put it on loud.

You wouldn't feel like coming round later, would you?

I know it always works out that way, Ken.

I hear it's a wonderful picture. You see it and then you can tell me about it later, eh?

No, I'm not being a 'noble martyr'. I'm just wishing I could go with you ... I'm just feeling a bit ... I dunno.

No, I *can't* go, Ken.

I asked Letty to come over and sit with him but she's got the kids and Frank and it's a hellova way over here and they do take him out driving in the car on Sundays. I put him first because I have to. But you know what I feel about you.

Look, if we could afford a housekeeper we'd have a housekeeper.

It won't go on for ever, love.

What did you say?

Well — maybe it is best not to try and meet, then — if that's how you feel.

It won't bring me to my senses, Ken.

I'm not doing this because I *want* to . . . I'm torn in two all the time. Because I love you and because although he drives me wild I've got to look after my father. Because he's old and ill. And I'm fond of him — even when I want to scream because he's so slow and so difficult and so *maddening*. Because I can remember when he was younger and he was funny and he made us laugh and it was good fun being with him and I can't just go off and leave him.

I expect it is bloody hard on you.

Well — there it is then.

Don't let's talk any more, Ken. It's no good talking.

I may sound funny. I don't feel funny.

I must go Ken.

OK, Dad, I said I'd come when the kettle was ready.

OK, I'll bring you your toffees.

I must go Ken.

Because he *needs* me.

All right I will *go* and be a little ray of sunshine.

It's a good idea.

Thanks. Thank you, very much.

(*She puts down the receiver*)

Oh, God. Oh, God. Oh, God.

Yes, I *was* on the phone.

It was Letty.

She'll be over for you on Sunday.

Same as usual.

I AM getting your tea . . .

1959

175

Shirley's Girl Friend 2

Picnic Place

Shirl, havin' a holiday is hard work, isn't it? You need a holiday to get over a holiday. Me and my boy Norm — you know my boy Norm? The one that drives the lorry with the big ears. Well, him and me went on a holiday. It was only a one-day outing really, but it felt longer. We went with Norm's friend Arnold and his wife Haze. They got a nice new car. Well, it's not *new*, 1944 model, but it is nice. They took Norm, and Norm's Mum and Arnold's Granny — that's old Granny Grigson, marvellous old lady. Got all her facilities. She can fathom anything. And then there was Haze and the baby, and young Charlie, and Rover the doggie, and me. Not bad for a four-seater.

Well, after we been going about two hours we start to look for a place to have the picnic, see. And Norm's Mum says, 'Oh look, there's a nice place,' but we got past it before we seen it. And then Norm says, 'How about there?' but it was only a field, so we didn't take no notice. And we went on and on, and after a bit I says to Arnold, 'If we don't stop soon we're going to get to the end of our tether.' So he says, 'OK, top of this next steep hill we'll stop.' And we did.

Me and Haze run up the bank to see if it looks nice

and it does. There's a view one way — not too much to worry you. And a little river with all pretty white detergent fluff on it. And then the other way there's all the traffic going by. Bus after bus. Lovely. Well, it's nice to have something to look at in the country. And you could tell it was a good place. People been there before.

'Come on,' I says, 'everybody out of the car. This is it. Bring the cushions, and the picnic basket, and the wireless and the macs and the sweeties and the Sunday papers. And don't forget Gran.'

She didn't want to get out at first.

Well, once she's got her shoes off she don't fancy another struggle. But we managed her up the hill. She's light on her feet, you know. Used to be a lovely waltzer. But she's very set in her ways. She likes to sit at home and brew over the telly. But it's not natural, is it? Haze says she don't give into her because once you give into her she's won. Oh, she is hard, Hazel. Got a concrete streak right through her.

Poor old lady. But she's ever so cheerful. 'Breathe in Gran,' I says to her. 'Do you good.' But she don't like the country. Can't get in the swing of it. Can't get used to the smell.

Well, we all settles down and has our dinner. It was Ready Quick Cheese Spread sandwiches, and Chummy Chew Choc Bars for afters. We seen it all on the telly — but it was disappointing. Didn't take long either. So we didn't know what to do then, so we watched a spider let himself down on his string and then we lost him. So we counted the aeroplanes going over — there's always more on a Sunday. And then the spider found Norm's Mum and sat on her . . . She didn't like it. 'Take it away — take it away,' she says. Well, she doesn't like wild animals.

Once a moth got in her nightgown with her. She didn't like that either. We had to slap her.

It breaks the monotony, though. But it's tiring, so we put the wireless on, so we could have a nice sleep, and all of a sudden Hazel says to me, 'Don't look now but didn't we come here in a car?' I says: 'I was under that impression.'

'Arnold,' she says, 'Arnold, did you put the brake on when we got out the car?'

And Arnold says, 'Don't you worry your pretty little head about the mechanical side of life. That's men's work.'

'OK,' she says, 'I only wanted to know.'

And he says: 'Why?'

And she says: 'Because the car's not there no more.'

And no more it wasn't.

We all gets up to have a look. Not a sign or a tittle of it. Well, the boys go off to see if it could of rolled down the hill in front of us, and we just sit there and wait and wait.

Hazel says to me, 'Where *are* we?' And I says, 'I don't know but it took us two hours to get here so it stands to reason it must be somewhere.' And Granny says, 'I'd like to go home now,' and I says, 'And so say all of us, dear, but we haven't got no car. Looks like we got a nice long walk.' And never was word spoken in truer jest.

The boys came back, faces long as Lent, not a sign of the car. 'Come on,' they says, 'it's walking.'

We got the cushions, the picnic basket, the macs, the wireless. We didn't bother with the Sunday papers. They was all blew about all over the shop anyway.

We walked to a bus, then we got a train, then we got another bus, and another, and we fetched up home about midnight. And to crown it all the stiletto

178

heel on Hazel's white winkle-pickers come off, and she was Dot and Carry One all the way home.

And guess what? Next day a farmer found the car upside down not as far as from here to there, behind a haystack near where we was sitting. You'd of thought it could of blew its horn or something.

Norm says it was just as well we wasn't all in it at the time. But I dunno. We might of had our pictures in the paper if we had a been. He says: 'You keep your face out of the papers. I don't want to see your face in no paper. It's bad enough in real life.'

(He likes his women to be exclusive, see.)

Oh, he is nice.

1960

Dumb Friend

Flatty . . . come here . . . come here at once. Let go of Mr Plimsoll's thumb and come here.

I'm so sorry. He always welcomes my visitors for me. *Sit, Flatty. I said Sit. Sit. SIT. And stay sitting.*

So sorry. Other people's dogs are such a nuisance, aren't they? Actually he's a very obedient dog. *Sit.* Well, we don't really know quite what he is but we think he's part Labrador and part Spaniel — the Elizabeth Barrett Browning ears — I always says he's a new breed, a Spanralab or a Labraspan! But we don't really know, I'm afraid. All we know is that he is Number One Boss Man here! But don't tell him I said so.

Off the sofa, Flatty — let Mr Plimsoll sit down. He thinks he has Squatters' Rights. *Off. SIT.*

It's very good of you to come and see me. I think I have got something to tell you that is going to interest you. Very much down your street.

Do light up if you feel like it. Have you got a match? Will you let him blow it out for you? He loves blowing out matches. *No, wait, Flatty. Wait. Wait till Mr Plimsoll's lit his cigarette. Now blow. Good boy.* Rather a damp blow, I'm afraid.

Of course, I know you so well by sight. I've seen you at the chemist's and we both post in the same pillar box. But it wasn't until I saw you at my cousin's coffee party the other night that I began to think that perhaps you, too, are interested in things of the mind? Good. Now I must ask you . . . Are you interested in Extra Sensory Perception, Thought Transference, Telepathy, and things of that ilk? Ditto . . . very much *indeed* ditto.

Flatty, stop breathing so heavily. He does it when he's happy. *Sit.*

Telepathy is my thing. I've been doing some research on it with Ainsley Bruce Pedley. Do you know his work? He wrote *Mind Out — Thought Coming Through.* I'm afraid he's a bit of a giant. I've known him for years. Himself here is a bit green-eyed about him, silly old boy! *Sit.* Ainsley would ring up and say he was in the mood and then Mr Flatfoot and I — to give him his full name — *Yes, we're talking about you. Stop thumping — you're too noisy.* SIT. Well, he and I would plod along to Ainsley's place, and then Ainsley would go into one room and I'd go into another and he'd transmit messages through the wall to me. But we didn't get very encouraging results. Well, I always got the same message. It was quite simple, just two words: Go Home.

The interesting things is that he hadn't sent it. He sent me lots of other images — cup and saucer, five of clubs, threepenny stamp. I didn't get a sign of them. But what I got was 'Go Home', so go home I went. Himself here was very glad when I did. Jealousy is so ugly, isn't it?

(Don't look now but Flatty likes you. He only leans on people he likes. Don't worry about the hairs. They brush off in two twos. Do you think you could tell him you like him back? He's rather sensitive.) *Good boy.* Sit.

Now this is what I wanted to tell you about:

181

Recently I got hold of a telly-whizz goggle box. Sorry. Television set, and himself and I are very keen on it, *aren't we Flatty?* SIT. And he is particularly keen on the commercials. There's a biscuit he's mad about: 'Crash, the Cooky that Crumbles — Crash Crumbs and Taste the Sunshine'. Rather far fetched, of course.

Flatty, don't dribble on Mr Plimsoll's shoe. It's horrid. Stop it.

It's the thought of the Crash Cookies you see. He can anticipate when they are coming on the TV and he sits there in front of the set trembling and making little M'm M'm sounds. *Yes you do. M'm, M'm. There's no need to do it now.* And when the Crash commercials come on he goes absolutely bonkers. Round the room, tail lashing, barking, and then when it's over, total and utter collapse. He's a completely spent dog, terrible to see.

I do hope you like dogs — you don't mind him on your lap? He is a bit on the large side. Yes, they do take a bit of getting used to. *Come here, Flatty, and sit by me. Quiet. Sit.*

Well, one day I had him on the lead, because he's an awful duffer in traffic — *down* — and he insisted on taking me into the self-service supermarket and dragging me straight over to the biscuit counter — *down* — where he leaped high into the air and retrieved for me a king-size carton of Crash Cookies. Well of course I had to buy them after this. *Down.* They weren't in terribly good shape. He doesn't always know his own strength. And then, he insisted on carrying the thing home and it was far too big for his mouth, wobbling all over the place. And this has been going on for weeks. I can't get him past the supermarket and the house is full of Crash.

No, I don't want to shake hands with you. All right, go and sit with your new friend.

I've been worried to death. In an awful tizz. Couldn't understand it. And suddenly I've tumbled to it.

You know what's happening, don't you? The television advertising people are working through dogs and he is one of their agents. And, of course, it was his superior intelligence that sent me those 'go home' messages at Ainsley's, wasn't it.

Do look, he thinks you want to go home! He's trying to drag you to the door. *Let go of Mr Plimsoll's thumb, Flatty. Let go.* He loves thumbs. Just wipe it anywhere. Oh, must you really go? I've got lots more to tell you. There's no hurry . . . don't run away Mr Plimsoll.

Flatty stop thumping your tail. You must stop sending people messages. You are not to do it — not to do it — not to do it.

All right, I'll take you back to the supermarket.

Flatty. *Come here.* Stop thumping your tail. Have you been sending messages again?

1962

Speeches

*There are certain phrases that, when you
hear them, strike dread in your heart. One
of these is: 'Do you mind if I say something?'
And another is the patent lie: 'I'm not going
to make a speech'. I would like to give you
three examples of this last untruth.*

1

I'm not going to make a speech but somebody has got
to propose the health of the bride and groom and
yours truly, as best man, has been detailed to under-
take the onerous task.

I've known Cuth since we were both knee high to a
grasshopper — or to put it in another way — ever since
Big Ben was a watch. And I can vouch, as can many
another colleague who frequents the Mucky Duck . . .
or, as perhaps we should say on an occasion like this,
The Black Swan Hotel. We can vouch that Cuth is a
bang-on player of darts and now we have the lovely
bride, the beautiful June, and she can vouch that he is
also a bang-on slayer-of-hearts!

So before we have another go at the buffet — and I
understand the trifle is not to be trifled with and the
bubble is gen-u-ine Widow Cliquot — (no expense
spared), I would ask you all to give three cheering
rows for the cappy hupple!

June and Cuth — long may they reign.

1962

2

(best county voice)
I'm not going to make a speech but I've been asked to
announce that the prize for the most original exhibit
in the show goes to Mrs Trigmont for her tiara made
from metal milk-bottle tops.

The knitting trophy, for a baby's dainty lacy shawl,
goes to Mrs Trigmont.

The baking prize, for a cake in the shape of a space
rocket, is won by Mrs Trigmont.

The carpentry-class-in-handwork prize for a pair of
'His' and 'Hers' television tray-tables goes to Mrs
Trigmont.

The County Shield for an arrangement of fruits
and flowers of the hedgerows in an unusual container goes to Mrs Trigmont. She used hips in a little
ketchup bottle.

We would like to congratulate Mrs Trigmont and
we would like to ask Mr Trigmont to give her our
good wishes for a speedy recovery from her total
collapse.

1962

3

Lady Clutch — Mr Mayor, Ladies and Gentlemen and Friends. I'm not going to make a speech but as the President of the Maisie Comley Whittaker Sunset Home Foundation Trust I know you will all want me on your behalfs — behalves — behalfs? — to thank Lady Clutch so, so much for so very kindly coming down at the very last moment and stepping into the breech, as it were, to rescue us from the abyss by opening the new wing for us today. (*Turns to her*) It is so, *so* kind of you and I can't tell you *how* grateful we are to you. We really are. It's quite wonderful. I can't tell you . . .

As you know we had hoped that Mr Fred of the Flybuttons Pop Group was to have opened the new wing for us but, alas, he has had to fly out to Helsinki to represent Great Britain at a Pop Festival and of course we wish him very well but we are so, *so* grateful to Lady Clutch for getting us out of a hole in this wonderful way.

Thank you so much.

There are a great many thank yous to be said today and we are particularly grateful to all those generous people who have given us of their old furniture, and *objets* and curtains that they no longer want in their own homes. I'm sure these are quite going to transform

186

the new wing.

And Lady Clutch has not come empty-handed. She has brought with her what she very modestly describes as 'one of my poor little daubs'. But, at the risk of being rude and flatly contradicting her, I must say I think it is an enchanting impression, in oils, of a herbaceous border in full flower at the very height of its summer glory . . .

It's a football match?

How stupid of me.

Of course, it's *much* more fun that it should be a football match. Thank you so very much.

I must also thank Mrs Harding and her cohorts of willing helpers who have done such miracles to make today possible. They are entirely responsible for the delicious tea I'm sure we are all going to enjoy later. Thank you, Mrs Bude, Mrs Lumpley, Miss Cordle, Mrs G. Elphase, Mrs M. Elphase, Janice Bednick, Morwenna Hanks and Sister Bunn. Thank you all *so* much.

Now, I cannot pretend that we are not very disappointed that the new wing is not absolutely ready to be opened today, but we do congratulate the builders, Messrs Clutby and Son for very nearly having it ready. And we are so grateful that the recreation and TV lounge *is* very nearly ready — except for the glass in the windows, because where would we all be without it? I think none of us expected hail.

And I do have good news. Messrs Clutby and Son have promised that, when the first of the new residents arrive to move in next week, the stairs will be there.

1962

Shirley's Girl Friend 3

Foreign Feller

Shirl, I like getting a postcard better'n a letter, don't you?

Well, you don't know what's in a letter till you open it. But there's not the worry with a postcard. I had a nice coloured picture postcard from that foreign feller I met last summer. Remember?

I told you. Well, you know my boy Norm? You know, the one that drives the lorry with the big ears. Well, he was a bit funny about me knowing this Heinrich, but I tell him we got to have hands across the water nowadays and he says: 'Mind you don't fall in.'

But I tell him not to worry. I got built-in water wings.

Well, I met this Heinrich in the post office. He was trying to post a letter and he didn't know how, see, so he says to me: 'Please is here vere I am for stamping?' So I says: 'No, here is where you are for your TV licence and your old age pension.' I say: 'You see that nice looking young lady over there getting something out of her tooth? Well, if you was to ask her very nicely,' I says, 'she might kindly deign to sell you a stamp.'

So he says: 'Please, you come vis me.' So we goes over and has a nice little wait and then she kindly deigns! and I am just going but he says: 'I am a visitor to London. You are very cordial. Perhaps you are the precious key to the stone portal set in a silver sea.'

I says to him: 'I bet you say that to all the girls.' But he says he don't know no girls in England. No, what he is passionate for is National Art treasures, oil paintings and that. I tell him we're being ever so careful of them now.

He says: 'Please you can tell me what is a must?'

I says: 'A must?'

Yes, he says, he read in a Come to Britain pamphlet that Hampton Court Palace is a must.

'Oh,' I says, 'it means you got to go there.' He says: 'Please vere is dis Hampton Court Palace.' And I tell him it's ... Oh, you know ... I mean everybody knows where Hampton Court Palace is. It's ... Oh ... D'you know, I couldn't seem to put me finger on the pulse of it, but he says: 'We will seeks it out together. You come vis me Saturday afternoon.'

I knew Norm was off on a run with the lorry Saturday, so I says: 'All right, meet you in Trafalgar Square, three o'clock, by the pigeons. And he takes me name and address down in a little book he's got and he asks me to call him Heinrich.

Because it's his name.

Well, I meet him, like we said, and he's got all little, short shorts on and he's got a camera round his neck because he's mad for taking snaps. It's religious mania with him. I mean, he don't just see something and snap it, like me or you would. He's got gadgets. He's got meters to tell him if it's hot or cold. I mean, you have to be a mathematical genius to understand it. Talk about Epstein. I mean, really.

Well, when I get there he is trying to snap some of them pigeons, and I says: 'Oh, come on,' I says, 'we got to go.' And he says: 'Eine moment, I achieve a jolly portrait of these doves.'

'Look,' I says, 'Hampton Court Palace isn't just round the corner, you know. We got to get there and it's a tidy stretch.'

He says: 'Pardon?'

I says: 'It's a hellova long way. If we don't start now we won't get there this side of Christmas.'

'Oh,' he says, 'I thought Christmas was a winter feast?'

'Look,' I says, 'don't pick it or it will never heal.'

He was hard work, I'll say that for him.

Well, we get to Hampton Court and he goes mad! He snaps the trees and the walls and the gateways and the statutes and all. I says to him: 'Don't you never take snaps of people?' I mean I wasn't looking too bad. I had on me chunky thick-knit and me pencil slim skirt. (It was last year, you see.) But he don't take no notice. Just says: Hold the meters, hold this, hold that.

I was fed up. 'Look,' I said, 'I brought you here to have a see but you haven't taken your eyes out of that finder. I've a good mind to take you into that maze I've heard so much about and lose you.'

He says: 'Please vat is diz Maze?' So I tell him it's supposed to be this clever garden with all high hedges you can't see over and little twisty paths, and once you get in it you can't get out of it and you're lost. 'Ho,' he says, 'that is a good joke. I will attempt it. You come too.'

But I says: 'Not on your Nellie. You're on your own,' I says, 'and if you aren't out in ten minutes you're lost. I'll wait for you here.'

I could see he was excited. His knees were twitching. 'OK,' he says, 'see you later, crocodile.' He wasn't with it.

Well, I go into the ladies and has a nice back comb of me beehive hair-do, and when I get out he isn't there. Half an hour, hour, and then the keeper comes along and he says: 'Everybody go home now. Closing up time. I'm going to lock up now.'

I says: 'You can't. I got me friend lost in your maze.' So he says: 'Get him out.' And I says: 'How?' 'Give him a yell,' he says. So I calls out: 'Heinrich.' But you feel so silly.

And that was the last I heard of him from that day to this, till I got his postcard today. It says: Thank you for your hand-clasp. All my photographs a success. That maze was easy. I came out in two minutes and had a big tea. Where were you? Heinrich.

Talk about hands across the water. I told Norm. He says: 'I warned yer. How are your water wings now?'

I says: 'Folded.'

1962

Stately as a Galleon

Music by Richard Addinsell

My neighbour, Mrs Fanshaw, is portly-plump and
    gay,
She must be over sixty-seven, if she is a day.
You might have thought her life was dull,
It's one long whirl instead.
I asked her all about it, and this is what she said:

I've joined an Olde Thyme Dance Club, the
    trouble is that there
Are too many ladies over, and no gentlemen to
    spare.
It seems a shame, it's not the same,
But still it has to be,
Some ladies have to dance together,
One of them is me.

Stately as a galleon, I sail across the floor,
Doing the Military Two-step, as in the days of
    yore.
I dance with Mrs Tiverton; she's light on her feet,
    in spite
Of turning the scale at fourteen stone, and being
    of medium height.

So gay the band,
So giddy the sight,
Full evening dress is a must,
But the zest goes out of a beautiful waltz
When you dance it bust to bust.

So, stately as two galleons, we sail across the
    floor,
Doing the Valse Valeta as in the days of yore.
The gent is Mrs Tiverton, I am her lady fair,
She bows to me every so nicely and I curtsey to
    her with care.
So gay the band,
So giddy the sight,
But it's not the same in the end
For a lady is never a gentleman, though
She may be your bosom friend.

So, stately as a galleon, I sail across the floor,
Doing the dear old Lancers, as in the days of
    yore.
I'm led by Mrs Tiverton, she swings me round
    and round
And though she manoeuvres me wonderfully
    well
I never get off the ground.
So gay the band,
So giddy the sight,
I try not to get depressed.
And it's done me a power of good to explode,
And get this lot off my chest.

Time

Music by Richard Addinsell

When I was a girl there was always time,
There was always time to spare.
There was always time to sit in the sun;
And we were never done
With lazing and flirting,
And doing our embroidery,
And keeping up our memory books,
And brushing our hair,
And writing little notes,
And going on picnics,
And dancing, dancing, dancing, dancing —
When I was a girl there was always time to waste.

Thank the Lord.

When I was a young woman there was always time,
There was always time to spare.
There was always time to walk in the sun,
And we were never done
With going to weddings,
Our own and our friends',
And going to parties,
Away at weekends,
And having our children

194

And bringing them up,
And talking, talking, talking, talking —
When I was a young woman there was always time
   to enjoy things.

Thank the Lord.

And when I was an elderly woman there was no
   more time,
There was no more time to spare.
There was no more time to sit in the sun,
For we were never done
With answering the telephone,
And looking at the TV,
And doing baby-sitting,
And talking to our friends,
And shopping, shopping, shopping, shopping,
And washing-up, washing-up, washing-up,
Writing letters, writing letters,
Rushing, rushing, rushing,
And we were always hurried,
And we were never bored.
When I was an elderly woman
There was never time to think.

Thank the Lord.

But now I'm an old, old woman,
So I want the last word:
There is no such thing as time —
Only this very minute
And I'm in it.

Thank the Lord.

1962

'It's Made all the Difference'

Is this seat taken? Do you mind if I sit here?

Thank you. Terrible weather, isn't it? I forgot it was early closing, or I wouldn't have come.

No, I don't live here but I came in on the bus. I thought I'd have a look round the shops and maybe go to the pictures but it's an epic. I think you have to be in the mood for an epic.

We've had a bit of trouble at home and I thought I'd like to get out and make a bit of a break. I can't seem to talk to anyone there, so I thought I'd get out for a few hours and then go back on the bus.

I hope you don't mind me talking to you like this. I just felt I'd like to talk to somebody who doesn't know me, you know.

That's very nice of you. I won't bother with the menu.

No thank you, I don't want anything to eat. I've gone right off me food. I might just have a cup of tea when the young lady comes over.

No, I'm not lonely. I'm married. We been married for years. We got teenage children. Two. Boy and girl. Roy is the boy and Brenda is the girl. They're very nice. Not like you read about in the papers. I mean they're friendly. They speak to us.

Yes, they're both working. They've both got nice

little jobs but I don't know what's to happen now, though. Everybody's gone so funny. You don't know who your friends are. They're all there like but they've gone different. I think that's the shock of it. Even my sister . . .

I never thought it would be like this . . . and Arnold's friends are the same. He's got lots of mates but it's like as if they've stood back and they take the mickey out of him. Men can be very nasty . . . and it looks like we're going to have to move. No, we don't want to. None of us wants to. We like it where we are and Arnold's got the garden lovely. Roses. He grows lovely roses, does Arnold . . . and dahlias, but he's going to have to leave his job, you see. The firm has been very nice about it but the foreman said it wouldn't be right. He said it would be most unwise. So, we've got to move. I don't know where yet. Somewhere where they don't know us, I suppose. It makes me so wild. I mean, it's not as if we'd done anything. It's not a bit fair.

Why couldn't it have been something reasonable? But a £275,000 pool win . . . just like that . . .

Oh, no, we don't want to give it back.

1964

Shirley's Girl Friend 4

Music Festival

When Benjamin Britten invited me to be part of the festival at Aldeburgh in Suffolk in 1964 (the highest honour I ever received), I wrote this Shirl for the occasion.

Shirl, you ever been to a Musical Festival?

Well, you know my boy, Norm — the one drives the lorry with the big ears. Well, him and me got all involved in a Musical Festival last summer, all unbeknownst. Well, Norm's got this friend, Walter, who's a musician. He's a *professional* musician. I mean, he can do it even when he's not in the mood. He's on clarionet — by trade that is — but on the side he's got up this group. They're all record players. They play on the recorder.

Yes, I know it's kid stuff, the recorder. They done it when I was at school, but this Walham Green Recorder Consort Group is different because they only do unusual music. 'Little known rarities,' he was telling me. *Very* old music. They was dances mostly, galliards and that, and they got very old names like 'Lord Partelotte's Reluctance' and 'Catch Jenny Bending'. It's like old time Olde Tyme Dancing.

Oh, they do Modern Contemporary, too. They've had a piece specially wrote for them by a Frenchman, called 'Experience from A to B'. It's all on just the two notes, he was telling me. Very clever, you know.

Well, this Walter come over to Norm's Mum's the other Sunday on his way home from a practice, see, and he hears me do me whistlin'. Because I whistle all right. You know I won a talent contest doin' me whistlin' once, whistlin' the Sabre Dance (*whistles it*) by — by — oh, wait a minute. I used to have a clever way of rememberin' his name. *I* know:

Catcha choo-choo-train. That's it. Katcha-churian. Well, this Walter likes the way I whistle, see, and he gets all excited and he says to me:

'Can you read music?'

I said: 'Not so's you'd notice it.'

'Oh,' he says, 'you are deprived.'

'Well,' I said, 'I never felt the need of it. If I like a tune I can pick it up.'

And Norm says, 'You never know where it's been though, do you?'

So we all has a laugh, and then this Walter says: 'You whistle damn well.'

'Don't mention,' I says, 'it's just a gift from the gods.'

'No,' he says, 'you do. If only you could read the dots like any other fulfilled adult you'd come in useful to me.'

'Who?' I says, 'Me?'

'Yes,' he says. And he tells me this Walham Green Recorder Consort's been asked to go to the East Marshmere Festival of Music and the Arts to perform a very Elizabethan rarity called 'Friar Balsam's Repeat'. And it's got like this whistlin' echo part in it has to be done by the human whistle. And Walter says his regular whistler can't do it no more because he's had a tooth out. 'Do you think,' he says, 'you could learn the echo part in "Friar Balsam's Repeat" and do it at the

199

Festival with us on the twenty-fourth?'

'Why not?' I says. 'I might as well live dangerously while I still got all me choppers. Come on, Walt, when do we start? What's wrong with now? So I learn it. It's not difficult, you see. They do it first, and then I just echo it. And it's nice and slow. I like slow music — because it's more musical.

Well, I practise and practise on me own *and* I go once a week to the boys at Walham Green. And on the evening before the concert Walter says to me: 'What are you going to wear?' He says: 'Now *don't* wear nothing too swinging and with it, will you? And *don't* have your hair backcombed up so bouffant nobody can't see past you. And *don't* wear your tangerine blouse with your petunia purple two-piece, because none of them things looks right in a thirteenth-century church.'

'Finished?' I said.

'Yes,' he says.

'Oh,' I says, 'So it's in a church is it, then of *course* I shall wear me skin-tight tiger-skin drain-pipes and a bikini top — *if* it's in a church.' I say to him: 'Whom do you think I am that I don't know what's to wear on such and such an occasion! I am going to wear a very simple, snow-white, uncluttered, up-and-down shift.'

Norm says: 'Don't overdo it. I mean pure's pure, but you only got the one whistling echo. Don't take off or anything, will yer?'

'Look,' I says, 'if a thing's worth doing at all it's worth doing well. "Friar Balsam's Repeat" is seldom heard today and it's got to be good in sound and sight.'

So I wore me up-and-down shift. But I needn't of bothered, because I was stood behind the pulpit, so I would sound more like a distant echo. Nobody saw a

200

living inch of me. I might as well of kept on me plastic mac. Still, the concert was a big success. They don't applaud in church, you know, but you can tell when they like it. They breathe heavy.

And Walter was pleased with me. He said all my intonations was dead on every time. I'm not sure what it means but I think he meant it nicely. Norm says it was all right from where he was, out in the graveyard. Because he couldn't come inside, it made him nervous knowing I was goin' to do me whistlin'.

He said: 'D'you know what it sounded like?'

So I says: 'No?'

'It was just like a girl trying to whistle like she was a far away echo.'

He's a great comfort to me that Norm.

Oh, he is nice.

1964

Opera Interval

Bravo . . . Bravo.

(*Applauding*) Oh, how lovely.

Wasn't it heavenly?

Bravo . . . Bravo.

Isn't she marvellous? That voice. It really is celestial. And he was *so* good, wasn't he? The one in the middle. The one in blue. You know, the main man. *Lovely* voice.

(*Gets up to let people pass*) Can you manage?

Do you want to go out and mingle a little and see who is here — or shall we stay here and digest what we've just heard? All right — let's digest now and mingle later.

Do you know, I think that when I was very very young I heard Belushkin sing that part, only he sang it lower.

I must confess I got a little confused in the story, did you? I know she's a twin and there was a muddle, but I can't *quite* remember why she starts off in that pretty white dress, and then when she comes in again later she's dressed as a Crusader. It's probably a disguise. But one wonders why?

She's the daughter of the man in black, I suppose. The one who sang at the top of the stairs with that lovely voice. Let's look it up and see who is who.

'Don Penzalo, a wealthy landowner.' (That's probably her father.) 'Mildura . . .' that's her I think . . . 'daughter to the Duke of Pantilla.' Oh, not Don Penzalo then. No . . . 'The Duke of Pantilla, father of Mildura.' Well, there we are.

'Zelda, an old nurse.' Yes, we have seen her. She's the one with two sticks and rather a rumbly voice, remember?

'Fedora, a confidante.'

'Boldini, a bodyguard.'

'Don Alfredo, a general in the Crusaders.' Ah, Crusaders.

'Chorus of Fisherfolk, Villagers, Haymakers, Courtiers and Crusaders.' We haven't seen the Courtiers and Crusaders yet, but we've seen the fisherfolk, villagers and haymakers — yes, we have. They were the ones with fishing-nets and rakes and things.

You know, one ought to do one's homework before one goes to the opera. I've got a little book that tells you all the stories, but I never can remember to look it up till I get home, then it's too late.

Let's see what we have just seen:

Oh, it was a market place — I thought so.

'Act I. The Market Place of Pola.

'As dawn breaks over the sleepy village of Pola in Pantilla fisherfolk on their way to work join with villagers and haymakers to express their concern over the Royalist cause.'

Oh . . . *that's* what they were doing.

'Mildura pines for her lover, Don Alfredo, who is preparing to leave for the Crusades' . . . ah, there you are . . . 'and disguises herself in order to join him in Malta.'

Oh, Malta. Dear Malta. How I love it.

Do you know it well?

I used to go there a great deal when I was a gel, and one had such fun. I used to go and stay with darling old Admiral Sir Cardington Dexter and his wife Nadia. Did you know Nadia? She was a *little* strange! He met her in Casablanca! Yes, exactly. But I won't hear a word against her, because she was always very kind to me. Oh, it was such fun in those days. So gay. Parties, parties and more parties. Heavenly young men in uniform — white naval uniform, quite irresistible, and you know, honestly, one hardly noticed the Maltese at all.

Now. 'Mildura disguises herself in order to join Don Alfredo, but Don Penzalo' (I'm sure he's the one in blue) 'seeks revenge for a slight done him by the Duke and plans to abduct Mildura, whom he suspects of political duplicity, and flee with her to Spain.' Oh, Spain. Very *mouvementé*! Do you know Spain well?

No, Italy is my passion. *Bella Italia.* I always feel very hard done by if I don't get my annual ration of *Bella Italia.* It's so nourishing.

'Zelda, an old nurse, reads warnings in the stars and begs Mildura to delay her departure until the harvest is gathered in. Don Penzalo does not recognise Mildura and challenges her to a duet.' That's what it says: 'Challenges her to a du—' Oh, I am idiotic. The light's so bad in here.

(*Gets up to let people pass back to their seats*)

I'm so sorry. Can you get by? Ow — No, it's all right, only a *tiny* little ladder . . .

One really ought to come to the opera more often. I do love it so. My mother used to go a great deal. She loved it, and, of course, she was very musical. Oh, very. She had a most enchanting gift, she played the piano entirely by heart, well I suppose you could call it by ear. She never had a lesson in her life. She would go to an opera, hear it, and then come home and play the entire thing (oh, I'm so sorry, did I hit you?). She'd play the entire thing from memory without a note of music. So, of course, I grew up knowing all the lovely, lovely tunes one knows so well. It is such an advantage — one step ahead of everyone else.

No, alas, I don't play.

(*Sighs*) Now, let's see what the next act holds in store for us. 'Act II. The Cloisters of San Geminiani Cathedral.'

I wonder if I've been there. So many lovely *Cathedrale* all over *Bella Italia*.

'Mildura, no longer disguised (oh, good), is on her way to Mass with her confidante, Fedora, and Boldoni, a faithful bodyguard. Playfully she takes off her chaplet of roses and puts it on Boldoni, who laughs.' That sounds rather fun.

'Don Alfredo, forewarned of Penzalo's plot, arrives unannounced at the Cathedral with a band of Crusaders, ostensibly to celebrate the Feast of Saint Ogiano.'

Are you getting hungry?

It's a very long opera, three more acts. Are you sure you aren't hungry? I should have fed you better. A boiled egg isn't enough for opera. I do hope you won't wilt.

No, I *love* it. I'm afraid it's all food and drink to me. Oh, there the lights are going down — it's too exciting — I'm like a child at the theatre.

(*Applauds*) I don't know who the conductor is, but he's supposed to be very well known.

Oh dear, we don't know where we are, do we. Well, we do. We're in the Cloisters of the Cathedral of St Geminiano. (*Turns to hush other talkers*) Sh. Sh. Sh.

1964

Lady Tullett

The exception to my practice of working slowly and out loud happened one winter afternoon when Reggie, as always on a Saturday, had the television on to watch the sports programme. I do not like watching sport on television. For one thing it is so wearing. I run every race, jump every obstacle with the horse, and swim every length of the swimming-pool. I don't take part in football, I just recoil from it; particularly from the note of false enthusiasm in the voices of commentators. And I do not like massed men's voices singing and whooping through 'You'll never walk alone'. But Reggie and Virginia Thesiger are both keen television football-watchers. When they switch on I move off.

On this particular Saturday Reggie and I were at home, and I was lazy about going upstairs to my work-room, and took a foolscap block and pencils into the dining-room with the idea of trying to think up ideas for a forthcoming concert-tour. I said to myself in my mother's Virginia accent: 'What you all goin' do this afternoon?' and at once I thought: 'I'll tell myself a story about an old woman in a rocking-chair, sitting on the back porch on a hot summer's night in Virginia.' I gave her a companion, Charlotte, and began to talk and write down what I said in the voice and idiom I knew so well from my ma — the story of Lally Tullett, a young school-teacher who had played a big part in the narrator's life fifty years before. The 'I' of the story is a very old woman and, as she reads aloud a notice of Lally Tullett's death, it unleashes memories of a dramatic incident long forgotten but now alive and felt again. At the end, with the merciful perspective of old age, she lets go of past pains and returns to tranquillity, rocking herself on the porch on that hot summer night.

For the only time in my monologue-writing life I had the idea and the way I wanted to do it, and wrote it down then and there, 'in one' as it were; complete. In performance I never told this story in exactly the same words because it was a memory, unrolling itself in the mind of the teller as she told it, and it called for a free style. But the paragraphs and sequence of events stayed exactly as they were in the original script. Lally Tullett remains one of my favourite sketches though not my favourite character.

In her rocking-chair reading a local newspaper is an old woman. It is a hot summer night and she and an old friend, Charlotte, are out on the porch of her house in Virginia.

Lord have mercy, Charlotte, guess who's dead? Lally Tullett! Lally Tullett. Remember? You knew her din't yer? I thought you knew her! Taught school here. It was just after Dan and I moved here, I guess. Maybe it was before you and Andrew came. I know it was a long time ago. I think my children were only little then and Fanny had just started school and John was home and I think I must have been carrying Tuppy that summer. Yes, I was, and little Dan hadn't even been thought of. Lord, that's a long time ago. Must be fifty-five — fifty-six years ago. My Lord! (*Reads*) 'Miss Lally Tullett of 1574 Cedar Oaks Avenue, Gainsford, North Carolina' (never knew she came from down there) 'sometime schoolteacher in this city, died Monday.'

Well, well; and Charlotte she was older'n me. I never knew that. She was very . . . not real pretty but kinder interestin' lookin'. Sometimes she was pretty as paint and sometimes plainer'n hell . . . but you had to look at her twice. She had style. She had great big old brown eyes and she was kinder skinny but she had *style*. I remember she had a cream-coloured linen suit with white braid trim on it and a white shirtwaist. I craved that cream-coloured linen suit!

That *was* the summer I was carrying Tuppy and I thought he'd never get here. Lally roomed over at Mrs Hackett's, had that big room out the back, the one that keeps cool in summer, and she brought all her own books and pictures with her when she came. She was a great reader, and she could speak poetry and she was crazy about good music; but there wasn't much of that around here then. I don't remember anybody had a phonograph and the only person who had a pianner was Dr Kinton. He played real good. Crossed his hands and everything. Remember? He went over to Vienna to learn to be a doctor and while he was there he took pianner lessons . . . and when he come home he bought hisself a great big old grand pianner, and whenever he had any time, he'd play that old pianner. He wasn't married then. Summer nights, with all the doors and winders wide open, you could hear him clear up here. Just as well his house was set back some. I think you can have too much good music when it's only practising.

Want some more coffee? Help yourself.

Lally used to saunter up the lane to Dr Kinton's in the summer evenings and sit on the bank outside his house so she could hear him playin'. No, she wouldn't go inside. Oh, he asked her but she wouldn't go. She just wasn't sociable. Everybody asked her to their homes but she wouldn't go . . . and she wouldn't date anybody. They asked her. Oh, they asked her all right. She was young and pretty enough and there wasn't that many pretty girls around, but she wouldn't go.

The only place she ever came was to our house. Well, we're right next to Mrs Hackett's and she used to come and play with the children in the yard. And then she'd come in the house and she and my Dan would argue. Lord, they'd argue about anything: politics and women's rights. She was kind of radical and it riled him. No, I couldn't argue with anybody. I haven't the brains nor the inclination.

I said to Lally one day, 'Lally Tullett, don't you want to get married?'

And she said, 'Yes, Hetty, I do.'

I told her, I said, 'Well, you are certainly going about it in a mighty funny way. All the nice young men round here want to date you and give you a good time but you always say No. You want to watch it or maybe you won't find somebody to love.'

She didn't say nothin'.

I said, 'Lally, have you found somebody? Hell, Lally, who?'

She said, 'I do not want to discuss it.'

She was like that. Brusk. Closer than a clam. Well, sir, I was pretty damn sure she had her eye on Dr Kinton, and I didn't blame her. He was a lovely man, and she wasn't the only one thought so. I thought she was playin' hard to get but I didn't say a word. I decided I'd just sit back and watch it all develop.

Well, sir, it was a mighty hot summer, hotter'n purgatory, and I felt all tuckered out with it; and one Sunday we were invited to a big picnic party over at the Forwells'. 'Member the Forwells had that house where the Presbyterian Church is now? They had more money than sense, and that bow-legged daughter with the red hair. She picked up her skirts in a three-legged race and we all saw! Just as well she had money.

I said to Dan, 'You take the children and have yourselves a good time. I'll just stay here and be quiet.'

He said, 'You sure you're all right, Hetty?'

I said, 'Honey, just leave me be. All I want to do is get my feet off the ground and get towards having this little old baby born.'

So they went off and I went up to my bedroom and I took off my dress. I took off my corset and I put on a thin wrapper and I lay down on my bed. It was the same old four-poster bed I still sleep in. (Used to be Dan's grandmother's but I'm going to give it to my grand-daughter. Because she's crazy for it, thinks its antique. I don't know where she's goin' to put it in that two-room apartment, but she can have it if she wants it.) I must have slept longer than I thought for when I woke up it was dark and there was a storm going on! You never heard anything like it in all your born days. The winders were rattling and the doors banging and the rain was hittin' the winders like stones.

I was startled for a minute and I didn't know where I was. I got up and lit a lamp and closed the winders and fastened the doors. I felt like I'd come from out some long dark tunnel and it was like as if I was the only person in the whole wide world . . . and I was scared, Charlotte.

I remember I was standin' on the corner of the stairway by the old clock, and although the storm was making a terrible noise I could still hear that old clock tickin' . . . tick — tock — tick — tock — tick — tock. A might lonesome sound. And my heart was going about twice as fast . . . tick-tock-tick-tock. And then, all of a sudden, as if it was written in letters of fire on the wall, I *knew* . . . that Dan and Lally . . . don't ask me how I knew . . . I just knew it, that's all. I just knew. I didn't know what to do. I just stood there and I said, 'Oh, no . . . no . . . oh, no . . .'

And then Dan come home with the children and I made 'em go straight upstairs to bed. I didn't know what I was doin'. I was so shocked. I couldn't be sweet to 'em. I made 'em cry. Well, I got 'em into bed and I came downstairs and I said to Dan, 'What do you want for supper?' And he said he didn't want nothin' but a glass of milk, and I couldn't have forced a crumb between my lips with a hammer and chisel.

We went out on the porch and the storm had moved off some, but you could still hear the rain hittin' on the leaves. I was mightly glad it was dark. We sat there and after a while I said, 'Dan, I want to ask you somp'n. Are you happy?'

And he said, 'Hetty, I want to tell you . . .'

I said, 'Dan, don't you say anything that's going to make it impossible for me and you to get right back

211

where we are now.'

He said, 'Hetty I just want you to know . . .'

I said, 'I don't *want* to know . . . I don't want to know . . .'

I went upstairs to the bedroom. I closed the door and I went to bed. I couldn't even say me prayers. And Lord, it was hot. It was hotter than Tophet. And I was cold like I was a piece of ice . . .

I don't believe I ever saw Lally again . . . I know she moved away soon after that but I don't remember if I saw her ever again; and I don't think Dan did either. He never mentioned her name to his dying day.

Lordy, that was a long time ago! It was a hundred million years ago . . . I have *not thought* of Lally Tullett in all this long while. Lord have mercy . . .

Mmm! Lally Tullett . . . Mmm.

I certainly did crave that cream-coloured linen suit.

Do you know somp'n, Charlotte?

She never did get married . . .

1965

212

Eng. Lit. I

Two other monologue-characters came into
being through the looking-glass. Years before I went into the theatre I discovered,
by putting my tongue in front of my lower
teeth, I could alter my face into something
I would not want to be stuck with if the
wind changed. Speaking with my tongue in
this position produced a plummy, rural
sound, and I gave it a Buckinghamshire
accent and loved it dearly. When Bertie
Farjeon asked me to write additional
material for The Little Revue I made up
three different kinds of mothers — an
American from the Middle West teaching
her daughter a poem by Shelley; an understanding mother worrying about her sixteen-
year-old daughter's infatuation for a middle-
aged Portuguese conjurer; and a Buckinghamshire village mother with a funny face
whose little boy got a conker lodged in his
throat. About twenty years later I decided
to revive the village mother, now an old
grumbler, and I put her in a sketch called
'A Terrible Worrier'.

The second character appeared one night
when I was cleaning my teeth. I looked in
the mirror and curled back my upper lip to

make sure they were clean and gleaming. (My teeth are large as tombstones and it is as well to keep them in good order for they are noticeable.) It occurred to me that I had found a new face and I wondered how it would speak. It spoke in a clear, clipped, educated manner and what it said was crisp and to the point. I went into the living-room where Reggie was still reading and I said: 'This is my new monologue face,' and talked to him in the new voice. He liked it. She is my favourite character in my gallery of 'monstrous women', the wife of an Oxbridge vice-chancellor. She has no name but I know her well, admire her intellect and wit and am devoted to her generous assumption, like Clemence Dane's, that everyone else is as well read and informed as she is. There is not much of me in this lady. I wrote three sketches about her called 'Eng. Lit.'

The character speaks in the same shape of phrase and with an unexpected use of words, as did one of my dearest older friends: Hester Alington, wife of the Dean of Durham, born Lyttelton and therefore attractively eccentric and individual.

(My favourite character) The scene is a book-lined study with stone-framed Gothic windows. A row of small painted shields are ranged along the shelves above the bookcases. There are group photographs about the room, and over the door is a pair of crossed oars. The linen chair- and sofa-covers are made from a cloth designed by

214

William Morris. It is just possible they are
original. The speaker is the wife of the Vice-
Chancellor of an Oxbridge University. She
wears an elderly cardigan of which she is
fond. Her speech is Educated-English, well
articulated, but she cannot pwonounce her
Rs.

Interview

It's really very difficult to describe my grandmother.
She wasn't particularly patrician but she did look
very like the great Duke of Wellington, only rather
prettier. Just as well, really. You know, there is a
picture of her in the front of my new book. I don't
know — have you read my book, Mr Wimble? No, I
know it is so difficult to find time to read what one
really wants to. No, it is only since you have so very
kindly invited me to come on to your television
programme in order to discuss my book I thought —
you know — that you might just possibly have read
it. But I do know how it is.

Were you up at this university, Mr Wimble? Oh,
how very interesting. No, I've never been there, but
now I shall make a point of going . . .

I imagine the reason you have asked me to come
on your programme is because my book has won a
literary prize?

I thought so.

I feel, perhaps, in all honesty, that I should tell you
that I was quite unaware of the existence of the prize
until I won it. It was what you might call a surprise
prize! . . . but none the less delightful for that.

No, this is *not* my first book. I've written several.
Lives. They're all Lives. And the reason I have written

the Life of my grandmother is because she was a remarkable woman and I liked her. She lived a very long time, you know — and she never lost interest. She was what you might call *consumed* with interest till the very last gasp. And I think ninety-four is a goodly span — that is why I have called my book *The Long Result of Time* which I don't have to tell you is Tennyson. I expect you have 'Locksley Hall' by heart, and I very much wish I had.

Yes, she was very eccentric. Very. And I think we ought to celebrate our eccentrics. It seems to me they are getting rarer and rarer. No, I don't know where they've all gone, Mr Wimble. I suppose they have been ironed out. I must say there's one thing about my grandmother: you could not have ironed her out! Oh, no — she was far too hilly.

Oh, yes, indeed, she was intellectual. Very. She came from a long line of intellectuals — father, grandfather, etcetera. I suppose the nearest parallel to my grandmother's family was the great clan of Darwins and Huxleys, and like the Darwin—Huxley lot my grandmother's family were also very much concerned with Natural Science and Genetics. And my grandmother's own particular area of interest was in the world of very small mammals.

Yes, isn't it interesting.

She had a long and very close relationship with a small red squirrel — yes, indeed, with a bushy tail! No, I've never known a squirrel at all well, but my grandmother did. And I must tell you that as well as her very strong scientific side, she was also very much concerned with reincarnation, and she was convinced that this small red squirrel was in fact the reincarnation of a much-loved cousin, who had been gathered at an earlier date. Indeed she always called the squirrel

216

Edwin after this much-loved cousin, and I think you will agree Edwin is not a very squirrel-like name. I don't know what you should call a squirrel — Charlie, perhaps. Or if one had Greek one might call him Skyouros. I expect you have Greek. I've only got a little bread-and-butter Greek, just enough to go through Greece, but alas, in no way classical Greek.

Oh, hello, Mrs Finley. What have you got there? The evening paper? Kindly conceal it from me, dear woman, until I feel stronger and can surprise it later. Thank you. Oh, Mrs Finley — is there a favourable chance of your finding yourself in close proximity to a kettle? I think Mr Wimble and I are both very well disposed towards the idea of some tea. And something crunchy? Lovely.

Yes, my grandmother was a great dazzler.

Oh, no, don't let's talk about me. I'd far rather talk about my grandmother. Oh, dear, what sort of things do television viewers want to know about one? Likes and dislikes — yes, I've got some of those. Oh, yes, I'm *very* passionate.

Well now, which do I like best — men or women? I think it rather depends what for. I am more *familiar* with men. You see, both my father and my husband were Masters of Colleges in this university, and now my husband is Vice-Chancellor, and we have four very agreeable sons, so you see, it's men, really, men all the way along the line.

I don't know what I'd have done if I'd had a daughter, but the question never arose. I do have a very frilly little grand-daughter about whom I am prejudiced. I think she's rather too aware of her appearance and her clothes for one of only six, but I find her very fetching — very.

Clothes? Oh, yes, I like clothes — on other people.

Well, somehow they seem to suffer a sea-change when they get on to me. They look quite promising in the shop; and not entirely without hope when I get them back into my wardrobe. But then, when I put them on they tend to deteriorate with a very strange rapidity and one feels so sorry for them.

I tell you what I do like — *hats*! Could I, perhaps, wear a hat if I come on to your television programme? Alas, one of the things of which I am not possessed is an informal hat. I fear my hats tend to be rather purposeful. Oh, well, I'll have to ask my adviser. My adviser? Oh, that's my grandson, Edward. He's only eleven, but he is *very* wise and he knows far more about the world of today than do I, and I abide by his judgment quite considerably.

I may say, Mr Wimble, that when I told him you had so very kindly invited me to appear on your television programme he said, 'Go ahead, Gaga.' (With a certain deadly accuracy he calls me Gaga!) 'Go ahead, Gaga. Live dangerously!'

I must confess this advice has somewhat unnerved me, and it prompts me to put a question to you: Mr Wimble, are you very cruel to the people who come on to your programme?

I see. And do they *like* that?

Oh, it's the *viewers* who like it . . . I wonder if I should.

Oh, thank you, Mrs Finley, we'll come and consume it instantly. In the dining-room? Right.

Tea.

Well, now I do very much appreciate your kindness in asking me to do this programme. I shall certainly consider it . . . A thought has just crossed my mind. Mr Wimble, what would happen if I were to come on to your programme and I were to be very cruel to you?

1965

Bring Back the Silence

Music by Richard Addinsell

*We had a few restoring days, after the
wind-up in Sydney, at a small resort off the
Queensland coast. 'Downstairs' (Dorothy
Jenner) had suggested Hayman Island, and
got in touch with the manager of the hotel
there and told him we wanted to be as
quiet as possible. I added that we would
like a 'lodge' (it was a cottage hotel) well
away from the main building, please, and
safely out of range of bar noises, and of
one of my least favourite modern menaces
— piped-in music. This intrusion of privacy
is bad enough in America, where surely it
originated; but now the meaningless background wall-paper sounds have proliferated
all over Britain too. At that date it seemed
more difficult to avoid in Australia than
anywhere else I had been. So strongly did I
feel about it that I wrote a lyric, soon after
my 1959 visit to Australia, that Dick
Addinsell set to a march-tune.*

To whom it may concern I dedicate this song
That it may right a wrong. Oh, please

Bring back the silence, the silence we once knew,
Before unending music was unendlessly piped
   through
To restaurants and office, railway station and to
   store.
Take back the music we beg and we implore.
It pours into the Ladies Room
Through cleverly hidden vents,
It pours along the corridor
And into the Gents — (they tell me).
Bring back the silence to stairway, lift and hall,
For we who care for music do not care for this
   at all.

For you never can quite hear what the tune is
   they're playing,
So soft and so dulcet, so damnably dim
Is the unending toothpaste-like strip of sweet
   music.
Damn, who ever thought of it,
Oblivion to him.

So please,
Bring back the silence, the silence we once knew
Before unending music was unendlessly piped
   through.
We know some company and their shareholders
   now stand to make
A lot of lovely lolly but for heaven's sake
Bring back the silence to airports and to banks,
Bring back the silence and deserve our thanks.

1965

220

Hymn

Music by Richard Addinsell

Such peaceful thoughts my mind doth fill
Serene my heart today,
And sweet and calm are all around
And doubt has fled away.

So undisturbed the view I see
Unclouded is the . . .

(Suddenly struck dumb by a terrible thought)

I've just remembered something absolutely
    ghastly.
I forgot to go into the kitchen before we came to
    church and turn the
Gas off underneath the chicken bones I'm trying
    to make into soup.

I know exactly what is going to happen, all the
    water will boil away
And the bottom of the saucepan will get red-hot
    and fall on the floor of the kitchen
And it will slowly burn through the linoleum and
    set fire to everything

And my fur coat isn't insured and where are we
    going to sleep tonight?

I wonder if I was to make a dash for it, what on
    earth I ought to try to save?
Thank goodness I'm wearing my engagement ring
    and my watch.
I suppose I ought to try and save that drawing
    that just might be by Gainsborough
But I'd far rather save my old photograph books
    and my cosy old bedroom slippers.

Darling, I don't suppose that you
Went into the kitchen and turned
The gas off underneath the soup?
No, I was afraid you wouldn't have done.

A — a — excuse me — men.

I Wouldn't Go Back to the World I Knew

Music by Richard Addinsell

I wouldn't go back to the world I knew,
I wouldn't go back for a day
Though I like to think of the world I knew
In a far off way.
I only see the skies as permanently blue
And all the people that I loved
As young and handsome too.
But I wouldn't go back to the world I knew
It's haunted now and dead.
A different wind is blowing and who knows
    what's ahead?

There we were the lot of us,
The people I knew then,
Glamorous girls with flattened figures,
Glamorous bright, young men.
Safe, contained, and confident,
Madly cheerful, fearfully gay,
Certain youth would last forever in an even
    better way.
'Let's play tennis!'
'Oh, how topping . . . bags me play with
    Teddy.'

'Daphne darling, you look spiffing . . .
Service . . . are you ready?'

There we were the lot of us,
Thoughtless, spoilt and young,
When the sun was always shining and the
    lovely songs were sung.
There we were the lot of us,
Were we 'with it' long ago?
Did we think we knew the answers?
I . . . I . . . don't know.
But I wouldn't go back to the world I knew
I wouldn't go back for a day
Though I still like to think of the world I knew
In a far off way.

All that sun and all that peace . . . it must have
    been serene,
It must have been delightful when we were
    young and green.
But I wouldn't go back to the world I knew
Although the skies were clear,
A hurricane is blowing now!
But still I'm glad I'm here.
No, I wouldn't go back to the world I knew
It was selfish, small and tame.
It had to go — the world I knew
But it was fun then, just the same!

1965

The Past is Present 1

*Another woman from Virginia this one is in
England. It is a stream of consciousness.*

I must be the biggest living idiot on two flat feet.
Waterloo Railroad Station, London, England. 11.45
a.m. I'm a grandmother and, with time going at the
speed of light the way it's doing now, I suppose I could
be a great-grandmother before I know where I am.
But not yet. Praise be, Susie is only twelve years old.

I must be out of my mind. I haven't seen the man
nigh on forty years and the whole thing was settled
and finished with and a line drawn under it. I don't
know what made me do such a stupid thing as to get
in touch with him again after all this time. I do too,
though. Vanity. ' "Vanity, vanity," said the preacher,
"all is vanity",' and he was dead right. And curiosity
— I want to know what he's like right now.

(Charlie, you had no business going off to Munich
on this conference for a week and leaving me alone in
London with nothing to do so I have to go and call
up my past in this crazy way. You should not have
left me alone. You know I'm a fool.)

I don't even known if he's still married to that girl,
Stella? Sheila? or whatever her name is. I can't remember. I half hoped I wouldn't be able to find him
again but with a name like that — Bassett-Palmer.
Henry Bassett-Palmer. It's so British. Like something

out of a Wodehouse novel. He was the best-looking thing I ever saw in my life — nine-foot-tall and hair like a hazelnut. I bet he's bald as a coot right now.

And I bet I look a million years old and he won't even recognise me. I've still got all my own teeth, though. Every last one of 'em, thank Heaven.

My Lord, that was a miracle spring. The only other time I was ever in England. Everything was going on — bluebells and birds, primroses and fair weather, every single day.

Loveliest tree the something now is something
something on the bough.

Som'pn like that. Henry told it to me and I can't remember a word of it. I thought it was in my head forever. Oxford, England in the spring, and Charlie and I, newly-weds on a lecture tour, Charlie lecturing and me touring — goggle-eyed. And then I ate som'pn disagreeable in Oxford and had to stay on over for a week while Charlie went to Edinburgh and Glasgow and other points north without me. And I met Henry.

(Charlie, you shouldn't have left me then and you shouldn't have left me now. I'm a frail fool and always have been.)

But I *am* full of curiosity! And a kind of funny little excitement this very minute. I never knew that you could go on feeling this way when you are as old as I am! Maybe it goes on forever. There's a thought. Give me strength!

He had the most fascinating little stammer. 'K-K-Kitty you look m-marvellous in b-blue. C-come on out in a p-punt with me.' And I went. And we fell in love just like that even though I loved you, Charlie. Still do and always will. This was just som'pn extra, outside.

But I felt so *evil* and so wrong, and by golly, Charlie,

226

it was a mighty powerful interlude even though it didn't last but four days and then a year of secret letter writing.

In those days we didn't just go off with perfect strangers. I hardly knew Henry except through letters, and that was just straight self-indulgent luxury. I could enjoy safe suffering that way. And it was real suffering too, Charlie. I was torn into shreds. That was when I lost all that weight. I had the best figure for a while: I enjoyed that. But after a year I knew it had to stop and I wrote Henry not to write me any more, and dammit he didn't.

I was so mad. Then he sent us an invitation to his wedding to Stella or Sheila, or whoever she was, and I cabled back 'I hope you will be as happy as I am.'

And I was happy, Charlie. It was true, I was happy and vain. I was kind of relieved, too, not to have to be secretive any more. I tore up all his letters and burned 'em in a bonfire. I wonder if they were as good as I thought they were, full of poetry and a kind of pleasurable melancholy. You have to be very young for that. Charlie said: 'What are you burning?' I said, 'Rubbish.'

I never felt so noble in my whole life.

I've gained a lot of weight since then.

Wish I hadn't worn this hat. I wish I hadn't come. I wish I was at home.

That train ought to be in by now. I suppose I'm in the right place? I don't know where I'm supposed to be.

Pardon me, I wonder if you can tell me where I should be to meet the 11.45 train?

It isn't true!

Henry Bassett-Palmer!

My Lord, you are still the best-looking man I ever saw in all my born days. You look marvellous. I have,

227

too, changed, but thank you for saying so.

Isn't this funny. I can't believe it, Henry. Forty years later! Forty years. How many grandchildren you got? I can beat you by two. Oh, Henry — this is so extraordinary.

What did you say? Oh, where is she? Of course I'd love to meet your wife *Sylvia*. Oh yes, that was it, Sylvia. Where is she? In the red coat over by the magazine stand . . . She's lovely looking. Henry — just a minute — does she know about me? You *did* tell her. No, I never, I never told Charlie. You go first . . .

(Charlie, come on back from Munich. You had no business to leave me alone in London. I'm such a fool. I need you, Charlie — come on back . . .)

1965

The Past is Present 2

*School Reunion — Old Girls' Day — with a
sub-title:*
'Time isn't always a great healer . . .'
Lumpy Latimer is no longer young.

It is Patsy, isn't it? Yes, I thought it was. I don't
suppose you remember me . . . Heavens! I don't believe
anyone's called me 'Lumpy' Latimer for years. How
ghastly! Yes, indeed — 'Lumpy' Latimer *as was*! My
name is Clinch now — as in boxing! I married a man
called Keith Clinch and we're living out in Ken-ya —
we have to call it *Ken*-ya now, you know! — and
we've been out there for *years,* but now the children
are married and are *here* so we've come back. Yes, for
good I think. Oh I *know.* I'm going to miss the sun
terribly . . . Yes, I am going to the tea. Oh, do let's
have a talk then. Lovely.

Oh, hello, Miss Davison! Yes, that's right, 'Lumpy'
Latimer! I'd entirely forgotten till Patsy Marsh just
reminded me. Isn't it ghastly? Well, I'm called Clinch
now — as in boxing! Keith and I have been living out
in *Ken*-ya — we have to call it *Ken*-ya now, you know!
— but now we're more or less settled here. Yes, for
keeps. Oh, I *know.* I'm going to miss the sun quite
dreadfully. I'm going to buy myself a woolly vest!
Are you by way of going to the tea? Oh, do let's
foregather and have a talk. I'd love that. Goodbye,

Miss Davison.

(*Pause*)

I say, it is Wendy Plackett, isn't it? I don't suppose you'll remember me. Yes, that's right, 'Lumpy' Latimer. I'd entirely forgotten till Patsy Marsh reminded me. I haven't been to a reunion since the year dot! 'Lumpy' Latimer as was! Well, now it's Clinch — as in boxing! We've been living out . . . No, not in the Argentine — in Ken-ya. Yes, they are both marvellously sunny. What is your name now? Still Wendy Plackett. Well, it's a lovely name . . . (*Pause*)

Isn't that Freesia McSomething? Oh, what was her name — Freesia Mc . . .? She was in the Flo Nightingale Dorm. with me and we all thought her terribly glamorous because she sleep-walked and was marvellous at elocution. I've never forgotten her as King Lear.

Isn't that Mamzel? Isn't she *tiny*? I must have a word with her. I say, do wait and let's go to tea together.

Hello, Mamzel.

Je ne pense pas que vous me reconnaissez. Oui — c'est ca!

'Lumpy' Latimer! *J'avais tout a fait oublié mais* Patsy Marsh *me fait rappeler! Maintenant, je suis appeler* CLAINCHE, *Madame Clainche. C'est* très *gentil de vous voir, Mamzel, très.*

Isn't she nice? I wonder why we hated her?

Everyone seems to be going tea-wards, so perhaps we should go too.

Oh, there's Fizzy Wiggins!

1965

The Ferry Boats of Sydney

Music by William Blezard

In my 1963 and 1966 visits to Sydney I took a flat in a new block built right on the edge of the water on the tip of Darling Point. ('Surely,' wrote Leonard Gershe from Beverly Hills, 'it should be "Darling, don't point".') It was found for us by Bettina Welch, who had been my neighbour in Macleay Regis in 1959. Bettina is one of the world's most kindly helpers as well as being a good actress and a pretty woman. The flat belonged to her brother-in-law who travelled a good deal and was often away from home. From the big living-room where I sat opposite French windows leading on to a balcony directly over the water, there was an uninterrupted view of the harbour, almost as breath-taking as the view I'd had from the eighth floor at Macleay Street. It was from there, as I sat to have my breakfast and early supper from a tray after the show, that I watched the ferry-boats go by. They plied across the harbour, from suburbs on both shores, to bring workers to and from the business section of the city. An enchanting sight.

Sometimes, before going to bed, I childishly stood up in my dressing-gown and waved across the darkness to the last ferry of the night on its way to Manly. It was never close enough for me to see if anyone waved back.

On the last night of my final appearance in Sydney, at the old Theatre Royal, I sang a farewell song Bill and I had written out of sentiment and affection for the ferry-boats:

When I think of Sydney
It isn't the Bridge I see.
Kings Cross? Opera House?
They don't speak to me.

When I'm far away
It's the Ferry-boats of Sydney
That I long to see.
I can do without those new buildings on the
   sky-line,
Skyscrapers are not my line,
It's the Ferry-boats I am mad about.
The ride on the water — toys painted bright —
They glide across the Harbour from morning
   to night
To Taronga Park for the Zoo,
Mosman and Kirribilli,
In darkness they look like harmonicas at sea,
Windows full of light.
It's the Ferry-boats of Sydney mean Sydney to
   me.

1965

A Terrible Worrier

Scene: the small and cosy kitchen living-room of No 2 Alma Cottages, Bull Lane, in a rural village in Buckinghamshire. Mrs Moss lives there. Her crony, Mrs Ingstone, from No 1 next door, is a mite hard of hearing.

There he is, Mrs Ingstone. That's his car. I'd know it anywhere. It is good of him to come round so soon. Look, dear, you let him in — I know it's my cottage but you're nearest the door, and I feel funny.

Oh, there you are, Mr Molder. Come in. You know Mrs Ingstone? I was just telling her it's very good of you to come round so soon. Now, where will you sit? Will you be all right on the settee? I think it's nice for a big man. Don't sit on Kipper!

You silly old pussy-cat. Get up off that nice settee and go and sit up on your window-sill — there's a good boy. He likes to sit on the window-sill and purr through the geraniums.

It's ever so good of you to come round so soon. I've been so worried. *I haven't been able to sleep, have I?* I told her. *I told you, didn't I?* I haven't been able to sleep.

Mr Molder, I've done a wrong thing.

Well, we don't know how wrong, DO WE? It could be criminal, but you don't know, do you?

I know you've got to get back to your lawyers'

office, so I'll tell you right away.

The other evening I was sitting in here when two young people come round selling tickets for a raffle, and I took two. No sooner did I have them in my hand than I realised I'd done a wrong thing.

No, that's not *the* wrong thing I've done. Oh, I've done two. Well, a raffle is gambling isn't it? I don't like the idea of gambling — I don't mind having a go at hoopla at a garden fête or that — but a raffle is proper gambling. But oh! The prizes were *lovely!*

First Prize is a cruise for two to Madeeria — there and back. And the second prize was a cocktail cabinet with all beautiful crystal goblets. And there was littler prizes — a brace of pheasants and a rabbit, and boxes of this and that and all for ten new p.

I told Mrs Ingstone when she come back to her cottage next door that I'd got the tickets, and she said, 'Mind you win that cruise for two and I'll go with you.' We had a good laugh!

But then I started to worry.

Because I might *win.*

Well, they could make you go, couldn't they? No, I wouldn't like it, because a cruise is on the sea, isn't it? I don't like the idea of being *on* the sea. I don't mind looking at it from the side, but I wouldn't want to be on it. Well, I mean, there could be a bad storm and would there be enough lifejackets to go round? And would they expect me to undress at night? And what are you supposed to do with your dentures?

Oh, I did worry.

And then I worried about this cottage. It's a council cottage, you know, and they might think, well, if she can afford to go off on a cruise . . . you see *they* wouldn't know I hadn't paid for it. They might put up the rent, or the rates. I mean they could turn you out, couldn't

234

they? You don't know where you are with them. I shan't vote for them next time, whoever they are.

Well, the day come for the bazaar where they was going to draw the raffle, and I'd asked Mrs Ingstone to go with me, *didn't I, but you couldn't come, could you?*

She was going to a lecture at the Women's Institute with her niece. On hormones. *But you didn't like it. Did you?* Well, they're not very nice, hormones. But did you know we was all supposed to have them? It was news to me. I don't think I've got any.

Well, I thought to meself, I'll just pop down on the bus to the Town Hall where the bazaar was and I'll just pop in and see them draw the raffle and then pop off home again on the bus. But when I get to the door of the Town Hall there was that Mrs Amblecrumbie or whatever she's called — you know, that lively little woman with the short legs, goes to St Luke's. She spots me and she says, 'Oh it's one of my Old Age Pensioners from the club. Let her in half price.' You don't mind the half price, but you don't like the attention being drawn. Still, I got a nice place up by the platform so I could see it all going on. A woman come on to do the draw, and she makes a great palaver of it, muddling up all the little ticketty bits in a container and then she puts her hand in and makes her selection.

'First prize — a cruise for two to Madeeria.'

She took all day undoing it, and I thought to meself — get on with it.

Then she opens the ticket and says, 'First Prize, Lady Clutton-Taylor.'

Lady Clutton-Taylor! Well — she can afford to go on a cruise any day of the week. Nobody much clapped.

I didn't know whether to laugh or cry. I was disappointed and relieved at one and the same time. I was just bending down to pick meself up to go home

235

when I heard my name called.

'Mrs Moss, 2 Alma Cottages, Bull Lane, a lovely rabbit.'

I looked up and there was this woman standing on the platform with a rabbit in her hand — dead — but still in its fur. Oh, I thought to meself, I'm not going to be bothered with *that,* so I won't say nothing. I'll just sit here, numb. But that Mrs Amblecrumbie . . .

'Bravo, Mrs Moss, you've won a lovely rabbit.'

Mr Molder, I had to get up out of my seat in the body of the hall and go all the way up to the platform to receive this said rabbit, and as she put it into a carrier bag for me to take off home I could see it had still got its eyes open.

No, I did *not* want it. Because you had to *do* a rabbit. No, I've never done a rabbit. Perhaps it is funny for a country woman never to of done a rabbit. Mark you, I've seen many a rabbit done. My mother must of done twelve a year if she did a dozen, and you'd be surprised what goes on under all that fur.

Well, I'm on the bus now, and I'm worrying all the time. How am I going to get rid of this blessed rabbit? I couldn't leave it on the bus because some nosey parker would come running after me, 'Oh, you've left your rabbit on the bus.' And I couldn't drop it into the gutter because it was raining. And I couldn't put it in my bin because they'd cleared it that morning, and you know what they are — once a week — if that — because they please themselves nowadays.

Oh, I did worry.

Well, I'm off the bus now, walking up Queen's Hill, and I pause to get my breath. I notice I'm standing alongside a little red car. It was parked, like, up against the kerb and its window was open about eight inches. And before I knew what I was doing I'd posted that rabbit.

As I done so a young man is coming down the hill and he says 'Good evening' to me so I know he's seen me do it. I say 'Good evening' back at him and I wait till he's out of sight and then I try the door. Locked!

I couldn't get me rabbit back.

I went up home and I didn't sleep one wink all night, DID I? I told her. *I told you, didn't I?* Not one wink, and at first light I'm down there and the car is gone. And that's the wrong thing I done, posting that rabbit. Mr Molder, what I need to know is this: Was it an abuse of personal, private property and could any person inform against?

You don't think so?

But are you sure?

Well, that's all right then. *You won't have to come and visit me in Dartmoor, will you?*

Kipper. Don't you dare scratch that nice white paint.

No, don't move, Mr Molder. I'm going to put the kettle on and we'll have a cup of tea. He has to go out a lot now. Don't you? He's an old boy. But he knows what he's going out for, and he's going to be quick about it because it's cold out there. That's a clever boy. You hurry up and then we'll have a nice cup of tea.

1967

Eng. Lit. II

An Event

The scene as before.

Mrs Finley dear, we are out of the dining-room at long last, thank you so very much. And that was a most triumphant repast. Oh, Mrs Finley, when the time is ripe for you, we are in the market for some coffee — in here if you can manage it, thank you so much.

Now, my dear nephew, sit you down somewhere comfortable.

Yes, that really was a *very* triumphant meal.

Oh well, you see Mrs Finley has only just come to terms and made friends with our new electric cooker. It has rather a number of knobs, and it really is rather daunting. One feels one is piloting a spacecraft. And for a while Mrs Finley only dared to be a Daniel about a knob called Simmer, so we had to make do with rather many meals of a tepid nature. But, now, if you see what I mean, things are hotting up, as it were.

If you are in the mood for a peppermint they are in the tin marked Edinburgh Rock. No, thank you very much. I shall try to resist.

It's very good to see you in our midst again, my dear John. How is progress doing in Africa? Oh good. One hardly dares to ask that question, for I so rarely like the answer. Progress everywhere today does seem to come so *very* heavily disguised as Chaos.

Oh John, do me a kindness and keep your eye on the time for me. There is a programme on the television that I *would* rather like you to see. It's not in the least important and we need not let it distract us unless we want it to. Perhaps you'd rather not? It's at 8.30, I think.

Oh, it's just a programme to which I faintly contribute.

Didn't you know I'd taken to going on the telly? Well that's an overstatement. I've been on it *once*. Yes, when my book about my grandmother won a literary prize. Yes, it was rather fun. This is my second venture.

There is no doubt about it, flattery does get one somewhere, and it got me on to the television. And for a while I was in grave peril owing to the great size of my head. Well, because everyone was so very nice to me and the young man who did the interview was very encouraging and so pretty. He had lovely clean hair, and he had on a psychedelic tie and, what's more, he treated me almost as if I were his equal. So you see it was very over-exciting.

Oh, the programme? It's a sort of discussion programme between so-called 'intelligent people' — they get you together and then they throw you a topic.

Oh, such as 'Infidelity'. Always very popular they tell me. And 'Is Happiness Wrong?'. I don't think it is, do you? No, I rather like it.

Now and again I did find myself a little out of my depth. Well, I know so little about Elementary Sex in Schools — or was it Sex in Elementary Schools? I can't remember now, but I thought it rather a bore.

Yes, I did enjoy doing the programme; only after-

239

wards the producer said to me, 'You are *so* natural,' as if there was a possible alternative. I felt as if I must have erred in some way; and I now feel a little self-conscious about the whole thing and I do rather dread seeing it. And I may tell you that is why I accidentally-on-purpose forgot to tell my husband, the dear Vice-Chancellor, this morning that his exhibitionist wife was going to be on the telly tonight. Because I do *not* wish to shame him in any way.

No, he won't remember. He only remembers Events if they are written down on his little Memory Jogger Pad by his remarkable secretary, Mrs Brittle. She does all his Event-remembering for him, so he doesn't have to bother.

He's dining with the Bursar — did I tell you? They've got some university business on hand. Protest, no doubt. It usually is.

The other people on the programme were tolerably agreeable. I think they were all very well known — except to me. You know there has to be something called a Fair Balance, so if you have a Labour then you have to have Tory — and we had one of each; one thick and one thin. And then if you have a man of Science, say, for special knowledge, then you have to have a Light Relief in the shape of a TV personality, and we had rather a crack-pot charmer of Scottish origin, dressed a little unusually, I thought, for one so deeply wedded to Caledonia.

Well, he was wearing an Arab burnous. No, it was never explained; nor was his relief *all* that light, come to think of it.

And if you will forgive a Laurentian joke — he wasn't much of a Pillar of Wisdom either!

Oh, I was there as a *woman*. There always has to be a woman for reasons of provocation and/or commonsense and, alas, I think I know which I was there to represent.

But, of course, *the* star of the whole thing was Dr Barstin. He's always on the programme, and you know all about him.

My dear John, where have you been? Oh yes, of course, Africa.

Well, he is a tremendous egg-head and vastly knowledgeable about a number of things without which I have managed, through a long and happy marriage, to do.

Such as the High Density of Infra-Radiation of Contra Ballic Span.

Exactly.

He is also a very, very devout agnostic, than which there are few things more bigoted. (He's a little under privileged in a number of ways.)

Oh yes, I got on with him all right until I thought he got mildly out of control on the subject of animals. People do, you know.

Mark you, I like animals — in their right place. We have our dear old hearth-rug of a dog, Hengist — or Horsa — he answers to both. But I do not find them as much fun as people, do you? I prefer people for talking to and inventing safety-pins and for playing Mozart.

But Dr Barstin could not, or would not, agree. He looked at the panel very carefully and then he said that in his opinion people were always *much* less beautiful than horses.

I quite saw his point. But I did think it was a trifle rude, and I couldn't resist saying: 'What about Greta Garbo?'

And you won't believe the depths to which he descended. He said: 'What *is* a Greta Garbo?' Laughter in court.

Can you believe it? I said: 'What a very sheltered life you must have led, Dr Barstin! You sound just like a comic magistrate in an old Ealing comedy.'

Yes, it did go down very well. There was considerable mirth. But Dr Bastin didn't like it, and he made a very cross face at me. I'm rather looking forward to seeing his cross face. Oh, is it time? Yes, turn it on. There is a knob at the side. It takes a moment to warm up, before it bursts into flower.

I think you may not recognise me when I come on because I am most unnaturally tidy. They sprayed me with some gassy substance that reduced my hair to the exact consistency of a dried loofah. I am uncannily wispless, and it stayed rigid for days.

Yes, Mrs Finley? The telephone? Oh, how tiresome. Who? My husband? To remind me to watch the programme? *Dear* man. How very nice of him. Will you please tell him I had *entirely* forgotten about it and thank him very much for reminding me. Come back and see it if you would like to, Mrs Finley, when you bring the coffee.

He is a *dear* man.

You realise, John, that Mrs Brittle must have put me down on his little Memory Jogger Pad as an Event!

1967

Good Old Jennifer

This is a story with a moral
And though it happened yesterday
It could also happen tomorrow —

From a nice simple home
On the outskirts of London
With a decent Dad and a Good Sport Mum.
And a dog called Monty and a cat called Tiger
Grew, in this midst,
Jennifer,
A girl uncomplicated by any silly nonsense.
There she was, tall and strong,
Keen on Chemistry,
Keen on tennis,
Keen on cycling and gym,
Keen on everything healthy.
She was always vaulting over hedges and gates and
    tennis nets,
And growing out of her clothes
And not caring a jot or a tittle if she did.
A great, big, bouncing schoolgirl,
Head of the Form, Head of the Dorm,
Good old Jennifer — Good old Jen!
And example to the Juniors,
A model to the Seniors.
Jennifer, Patrol Leader of the Daffodils
And a whizz at the High Jump.

Her mother said,
'Thank goodness she is so sensible.
Not bothering her head about perms and lipstick
And other sillinesses.'
'Thank goodness,' said her mother, 'she is so
　　natural and commonsensical.'
Things went on quite ordinarily
With Jennifer jumping downstairs three at a time.
And banging about the house.
And then her mother thought it was time she
　　calmed down a little,
After all she was going on sixteen.
And so when Jennifer was asked to a dance at the
　　Tennis Club
Her mother said she must go.
But Jennifer said she *loathed* dressing up and going
　　to parties
And *need* she? It was so much more wizard biking
　　with Betty
And Camilla and Joan.

But her mother was firm.
She bought a new dress for Jennifer in rather a
　　wrong pink
And had her hair done
And gave her a compact and a little bag
And silver shoes and some pale pink lipstick
And Jennifer went to the party.
She stood by the door in agony.
Her father danced with her first
And then her mother made her dance with the
　　doctor's son
Who wasn't much good but strong.
And then her father danced with her again
And then her mother grabbed hold of a boy who

was hovering by the door
And he asked Jennifer if she could do the
   Charleston
And she said, 'No.'
Then her father gave her another turn or two and
   they had ices.
In the dining room she saw David.
She'd known him since she was about five years
   old, only lately
He'd been away at school and his family had
   moved out of the district.

She said 'Hullo David',
But he didn't see or hear her because he was
   laughing with a
Long cool redhead in a frilly dress.
Jennifer hung around the dining room until the
   next dance was over
In case David should come back.
She thought she would go over to him and slap him
   on the back
and say 'Hullo Dave.'
But somehow when he did come back and was
   within striking distance
She simply couldn't.
She could only stand and stare for a bit and then
   go out into the
Garden and vault over the potty little low box
   hedge
And wish, for the first time in her life, that she
   knew how to dance properly.

She also wished she was much older
Or much younger
And a different shape.

She wished she was slightly delicate and frail,
That she was very graceful and about five feet two
    instead of being
Five feet eight.
She wished above all else that David would notice
    her.
But he didn't and she went home with her father
    and mother
And had a cup of hot cocoa and went to bed.
Next day she went to the Library to change her
    mother's book
And there outside on the pavement was David.
He looked at her for a moment and then said:
'Hullo, Jen — Were you at that dance last night?'
'Yes,' said said, 'I was.'
'Well, you might have said so. Did you see me
    there?'
Jennifer swallowed, 'No, I didn't actually.'
David said, 'I saw you in a sort of pink dress.
But when I looked again you'd gone.'
Jennifer's innermost wish was to jump over the
    hedge in the Library
Garden but with great self-control she stayed
    where she was
And asked David to come and play tennis that
    afternoon.
He came and she beat him in three straight sets.
She never saw him again.

1967

The Wedding is on Saturday

The scene is in a kitchen.

Anna? I'm sorry to bother you when you're busy . . .
I know you are just getting the supper. Oh Bryan,
let me in. Well, it won't matter if it's five minutes late
for once, will it?

Oh, Anna, do stop stirring. I've come to see you
because I need help and that's what sisters are for, in
case you don't know.

Anna! I am not dramatising. (*Sits*) Honestly . . .
well, all right then . . . I *am* dramatising. I think it is
quite dramatic! I'm not going to marry Alan.

Oh! Don't look so stricken!

I know the wedding is on Saturday and you've
been so marvellous about everything . . . my clothes
and the party here afterwards . . . and I know how
relieved you and Bryan were when you thought I was
off your hands at last.

No, Anna! That's not being ungrateful. It's just
being honest. I don't blame you. I've been hanging
around for far too long . . . But I can't marry Alan
and I don't know how to tell him. (*Gets up*) I think
I've known for about two days. He's away on business, up in Nottingham and he's coming back this
evening. Today was my last day at the office and I've
been tidying up to hand over to Joan Tidwell . . .
she's taking my job, you know? And all of a sudden it

came over me . . . this whole thing is a mistake. It's all a mistake and I can't marry Alan. I'm not panicking . . . I'm absolutely calm. I suppose when you're young, it's quite easy to get married but when you are over forty, to put it mildly . . .

Yes, I'm sure everybody will think it's *very* funny. 'Middle-aged spinster . . . does she know the facts?' Yes, she does, thank you very much. Personally! Yes, I do mean personally!

Oh, Anna, it was years ago and you wouldn't believe me if I told you. It was in the war when I was evacuated up to North Wales and you were in the A.T.S. in Swindon or Salisbury or wherever it was.

Yes, I was . . . much too young. Anna, I'm not going to tell you who it was. You didn't even know him.

Nor did I, come to that.

Or hardly . . . that's why I was such a miserable . . .

No! I didn't want to marry him. He was too young and he wasn't very nice and he wasn't very attractive. He was only sort of fascinating . . .

Of course I was shattered! I nearly died of guilt! It was agonising . . . and we all went home that Easter and I was certain everyone must know. They *must* know.

I've never been so miserable in my life. That was when I decided I was going to be a nursing missionary! It lasted the whole of a week. Oh! I got over it because you do . . . but I'm not very modern, Anna.

How am I going to tell Alan? Oh! Anna! Not about that. Anyway, he knows . . . I mean about not marrying him. I feel so trapped. Everyone is *so* pleased *for* me. Alan has sold his house and we have decorated the flat . . . and his daughter is just like you. She's so relieved to have got him off *her* hands . . . and Alan is so damned happy. Yes . . . I was! I know I was . . . but it's all gone now.

Hello, Bryan. I'm afraid your supper's going to be late. I had to talk to Anna. I'm not going to marry Alan. Look at his face! I know the wedding is on Saturday.

Yes, I'm sure everyone will think it's jolly funny.

Yes, I was mad for Alan to ask me to marry him. He's very attractive and I loved him. It was nice to be wanted. I've hated being on my own for so long. I nearly suffocated on my own for so long. Perhaps I've been on my own for too long, leading my own tidy little life in my own tidy little way and now that I have a chance to get away from it, it looks beautiful and orderly and safe and it's *mine*. And I don't know how to tell Alan.

Yes, Anna, I know it's my job.

I must go. I'm meeting him at the flat. We're supposed to be putting up the books; we've been lugging them up there every time we go ... 'His and Hers' ... and they're all over the floor. (*Looks at watch*) He'll be there now. I can just see him standing there not knowing where to begin! I hope that paint's dry on those shelves ... not that it matters.

I wonder if he feels like this? I hadn't thought of that. Perhaps he doesn't want to marry me any more? (*Long pause*) I must go and tell him it's all right ... it's all right ... in time it will be all right. I must be *dotty* ... I can't think what came over me ... *Swear* neither of you will ever tell a living soul that I came here this evening. Swear ... it never happened ... no, Bryan, I'll let myself out. It's all right. I do hope he's there ... I think he will be ... it's all right ... it is all right ...

1967

Unsuitable

Music by William Blezard

As you see
I'm over twenty-one.
As you can see
My gadding days are done.
Built for comfort, not for speed —
No need for me to tell you,
You can see
What's happened to me
What's happened to me — is maturity.

As you see
Frivolity is past.
As you can see
Solidity — at last!
Responsible, settled, pretty square,
There's no need for me to tell you
What has happened to me.

You can see
I'm a hat and gloves and pearls type
With a shopping bag on wheels —
Get the picture? Get the symbols?
I quite like how it feels.

But I do have a tiny problem
And I must confess it appeals
To
The other side of my nature:
I've a pair of Achilles' heels:
> I respond to the beat of rhythm,
> Rhythm, hot or sweet,
> I'm a silly old fool,
> Can't keep my cool,
> I go bouncy when I hear the beat.

I go bouncy when I hear the beat
And my well-gloved fingers snap,
I swing and sway in a groovy way
And my well-shod feet go tap.
I go bouncy when I hear the beat
In an olde worlde way maybe.
A middle-aged matron as you can see
In a middle-aged hat on her way to tea
But inside all hell is breaking loose in me.
I go bouncy when I hear the beat.
It's unsuitable — Heaven knows.
How long will it last, d'you suppose?
Time doesn't seem to remove it —
And I love it.
> I love it.
>> I love it.

I go bouncy when I hear the beat
And my dear old face goes pink
Standing in the queue when the bus is due,
The change in my purse goes chink — chink.
I go bouncy when I hear the beat
And I know that I look an ass —
A middle-aged matron — a pretty pass —

Senior citizen and plump, alas,
Bouncing about to Tiawana Brass —
I go bouncy when I hear the beat.

1967

Nicodemus' Song

*'Nicodemus' was unlike anything I had ever
seen on stage or ever written before or since;
and it was given to me on a plate. I was in
South Africa; friends sent their car to fetch
me to luncheon. Their driver was a young
black African of twenty-five. I asked him
where we were and he told me it was the
University. 'Education is a wonderful thing,'
he said, and tapped his forehead with the
heel of his hand. He had not been able to
finish his education because his family's
money ran out, but he told me he read many,
many books. 'What kind of books?' I asked
conversationally. 'I am finding W. Somerset
Maugham is more easy for me than Stefan
Zweig. It is in translation.' I sat up. 'What
else do you read?' 'I am finding Chekhov is
most poetical writer.' 'What else?' 'Guy de
Maupassant and others.' He belonged to a
Methodist Church reading club, where all
the members read the same books and dis-
cussed them later with the head man, who
was a wonderful teacher and read many,
many, many books. We talked of the possi-
bility of understanding through reading; of
poetry, of love. He said: 'I am going to many
places in books. All the time I am travelling*

in my head.'

When I got the chance (powdering my nose at my destination) I wrote down that last sentence Nicodemus had said before I forgot its precise wording.

Back in London I tried to make a song out of it and had the idea of using drum-beats as an accompaniment. I worked out a rhythm, two beats in the left hand against three in the right, slapped out on my knees with the flat of my hand. I read the lyric to Dick over the telephone. He asked me if I had a shape for the song in my head — a working tune? I told him about the drum rhythm and he asked me to tape the lyric with the drum-beats to give him an idea of what I wanted. When he heard the tape he said the piece had no need of music; it was complete, spoken against the drum rhythm, and I was to do it that way.

I first performed it at the Yvonne Arnaud Theatre in Guildford where Laurier Lister devised a lighting-plot that concentrated on my hands and knees and kept my face in darkness. I introduced the item by telling of the meeting with Nicodemus and explained that I had put his words into a formal shape, but the ideas were all his. I established the drum-beats, returning to the rhythm for the two choruses.

I must not leave my country,
I cannot get a pass to go away.
Money is something you must have also
And money is something I do not have today.

254

But I am making a discovery:
Right where I am, are books and books,
And books are full of people and places,
And wide new ideas and poems
On Love and other subjects
And I am going away, away
I am going away in books.

All the time I am travelling in my head,
All over the world I am going.
I am travelling in my head
And I am knowing
Different places
Different history
Different thinking
Different mystery
And people, people talking.
All the time I am travelling in my head
Making discovery.

Johannesburg is my city,
I drive a big car for a business man.
Waiting is something I must do often
And when I'm waiting I am reading when I can.
Since I am making my discovery
More I am reading books and books,
And books are full of terrible stories
And wonderful visions growing
Of man and all he can be
And I am going away, away,
I am going away in books.

All the time I am travelling in my head.
etc. etc.

1967

Eng. Lit. III

The scene, as before.

Mrs Finley, I'll be in the study all the morning should you have dire need of me. I'm about to plunge into an uninviting ocean of correspondence, none of it, alas, for joy, so I will welcome an interruption should there be a just cause. Yes, I'd love some elevenses a little later. About half past ten? But nothing farinaceous, thank you so much. No, I must be rigid.

(She turns into the room)

Oh, I am so sorry — I didn't know there was anybody in here. I'm the Vice Chancellor's wife and I expect you've come to see my husband and you've just missed him by a whisker. I am so sorry.

Oh, you've come to see me.

How nice of you — do sit down. Would you like to take your hat off? You are a young man, are you not? It's rather difficult to see under the floppy brim. I think it's friendlier to take it off, since we are in the house. Just put it anywhere.

Are you a member of this University?

And do I perhaps know you? What is your name? Mervyn.

Mervyn anything in particular?

Mervyn will do. Yes, I'm sure it will.

I must ask you Mervyn, how did you get in here? Oh, my husband really is *too* much the absent-minded professor — he simply goes through doors with never a backward glance and it does make for draughts. The insurance people are not at all fond of it. Nor am I. I must chastise him yet again. Did you by any happy chance shut it? Well done —

There's an ashtray just beside you.

Now what can I do for you?

You're from what? *Psst*?

I'm so sorry I'm afraid I don't know what *Psst* is? How do you spell it? P.S.S.S.T. — oh Pssst — yes. Does it signify something?

I didn't know we had an underground newspaper in this university! And it's called *Pssst*. That's *very* exciting. How long has it been going on? Two weeks! Triumphant.

I suppose it is fairly disagreeably destructive? That is it's function. Well I suppose it couldn't be all sweetness and light or it wouldn't have to go underground, would it? And what is your job in it? Editing *and* writing must be very demanding. What sort of things do you write about?

Total exposure — in every sense of the word.

And revolution — no holds barred.

I can quite appreciate the passion for frankness but I'm not so in love with the idea of total exposure simply because when all the impossibilities have been exposed and expressed where do we go from there? And in one sense it must be so chilly and rather taxing trying to keep a fresh eye on things?

Yes, I expect it is — b . . . . y hard work. Most missionary zeal is.

Oh . . . do lie down if that's how you feel but could you perhaps keep your feet off that little cushion. It's rather a special treasure — It was embroidered by a beloved great aunt of my husband's and we're so fond

257

of it. The violets are *so* pretty . . .

I don't know whether you know it or not but I write a certain amount myself? Books. Well, I write lives, and so far they have all managed to be about fairly agreeably constructive people — I find I do tend to tire very rapidly of sin . . . (There is an ashtray just beside you). Were you perhaps very kindly going to invite me to write something for your newspaper?

No. No. Why *should* you?

No, I don't mind in the least — it might have been a little embarrassing since my husband *is* Vice Chancellor and one has certain matrimonial loyalties . . .

Or did you want to expose me? I don't *think* I'm very exposable. I'm rather humdrum, I'd say. In fact I think I'm probably what I appear to be and that's bound to be a disappointment.

You don't want to write about me. Then . . . what is your problem?

Not selling enough copies. Oh dear.

Hard cheese. After only two weeks . . .

I must just ask you: what gave you the idea I might be, as it were, on your side?

Oh, when did you see me on the telly? I ask because I've only done it twice. Once when a book I wrote won a literary prize. Yes, it was rather fun. And the other time was when I was on a discussion panel with three party political men of quite astonishing boredom. I was very nearly deafened by the sound of axes being ground. Perhaps I said something memorably revolutionary?

Did I? I don't remember . . .?

You don't remember!

Nor do I. What then?

I give the impression of being 'gutsy'! Do I? I imagine that is a good thing to be . . .? Well, how can my gutsiness be of service to you?

(Quite rested from your lie-down? There is another ashtray just there . . .)

You want to get your newspaper banned!

Yes, it does sometimes boost sales to ban things.

But I'm afraid I'm not in a position to ban anything.

Yes, my husband is but you know he really isn't much for banning things. I mean he's not much of a Mrs Mary Westhouse, or whatever she's called — he's much more a Mrs Patrick Campbell. Oh, don't you know who she is? Everyone is too young now. Well, she was an actress of considerable renown and she is supposed to have said she didn't mind what people did unless they did it in the street and frightened the horses.

But I do see the value of a ban. Forbidden fruit is always more attractive. I remember when I was sixteen, and in those days sixteen was a very fragrant age; one was delightfully expectant of universally happy endings. I still think it's possible . . . Anyway I was forbidden to read the poetry of Algernon Swinburne, so of course I immediately obtained a volume of the poems of Algernon Swinburne and I read it with the utmost difficulty by the perilous illumination of a candle, within the confines of the linen closet and very disappointing it was too. Because I didn't understand one single word poor dear Swinburne was on about. Really we rather did know too little about everything in those days but of course one comes to it all eventually. You just go there and the whole of life arrives — I've grown quite tolerant of poor dear Swinburne, take it or leave it. Leave it mostly.

(Oh, did your cigarette quite make the fireplace? Good. I was just a trifle concerned about the hearth rug.) One would rather like to know what someone like Swinburne presently thinks of society today, wherever he is, dear man.

I don't believe in reincarnation, do you? No. I had a grandmother who did but I think it would be very unnerving to come back as a Peruvian tin miner or a stick insect. I'm very drawn to the idea of stick insects because they really are exactly like sticks, aren't they, and it must be so confusing for them — really, creation is *so* astonishing. Sometimes I get quite dizzy just thinking of a feather. Or Mount Everest.

(No thank you, so much. I don't take snuff. Do you find it pleasant? — Oh, God bless you.)

I suppose you feel it is *vital* that your paper should go on? I mean you feel it has much to offer for the betterment of life for us all? How do you see this happening?

Total anarchy!

You are *very* total, aren't you? I do see the charm of anarchy in the abstract but then I pause and think: who is going to be responsible for the plumbing?

Well, you *should* think about it, Mervyn. Drains and the disposal of refuse are central to the better life, I'd say, and people who want to clear away everything never quite think it through . . .

I wish I could help you because I am very keen on freedom and progress and other noble concepts but quite honestly I don't see them coming about through anarchy, and I don't think my husband would exactly cheer if I was to get involved with it all.

By the way, do you know my husband?

Well, you should. Because he's most frightfully nice and a member of the human race and I may tell you he knows a very great deal about anarchy.

No, not exactly pro, but fully conversant with.

Look, come to supper on Sunday and you can talk

to him about it. You can interview him for your paper. What's it called? How about this for a headline 'Vice Chancellor grilled by *Psst* —'. You could even surface from the underground and sell it through W.H. Smiths. It's a far wider market.

Well, all right don't if you don't want to.

Anyway come to supper on Sunday. You don't look very well-nourished to me. Have you had any breakfast? Well, you should have. It's a civilised meal. Our dear Mrs Finley, who looks after us so beautifully, is quite startlingly gifted with an egg and it would over-excite to a degree to be allowed to coddle one for you now.

Oh, come on, Mervyn. Don't be so surly.

We can't all be anarchists. Live and let live. We'll go and routle out an egg. And will you promise me something — when you come on Sunday, please wear that pretty suede jerkin — I love all those fringy bits. I mean it. It is an altogether superior garment and if I've got it right, you look very grooved in it.

1968

One is One and All Alone . . .

Scene: a tiny bed-sitter-cum-kitchen. No
teeth.

Well, it's ever so good of you to tell me about the outin' but I don't think I'll bother with it this year.

Where's it to? I been there. No, I don't think I'll bother this year.

No, I don't mind bein' on me own. I'm used to it. Got no choice, have you?

Well, I *had* a family. I had a sister; and I had a brother, too, but they been gone a long time. I got a niece somewhere — I think she's in Canada. Or could be in New Zealand. It's one of them places. I've got her name — her married name, wrote down somewhere safe. But she don't write and I don't write and there you are.

Oh yes, I *see* people.

The ladies come round on wheels with my dinner. Sometimes it's quite nice when it's hot.

And I've got a lovely young home 'elp. A 'ome help. She does me out lovely — gets the bed right out in the middle of the room and gets all the fluff up. There's always a lot of fluff under my bed. We don't know how it gets there. She says to me, 'You have made a lot of fluff this week!' We have a good laugh about it.

And she's got a very nice hubby, and he's handy with it. He just done up their lounge and he had some of the wall paper over, so he brought a piece round here and put it up on that wall. I like all those little Japanese pagodas. If you look at them at different angles you can see faces.

I see where the damp is still coming through.

Oh — my telly? I couldn't do without my telly. Somebody give it me. I think it was the Government. Or could of been the Red Cross? That type of thing. But it's got a bad habit. The pictures go over and over, like this, and you have to hit it. They sent a feller round and — he tampered with this and that and he got it lovely for about two days. Then it began again . . .

I don't like to touch it because it's electrical, you see, and you never know, do you? So I just hit it.

No, it doesn't happen all the time. Only every ten minutes.

Yes, it is a nice little room, isn't it? I'm very fond of it. Do you know if you was to lean out of that window you could see the back of Woolworths! I like to think of it going on there.

Yes, I keep nice and warm. I don't think you're supposed to but I light the oven and leave the door open! . . . It's *lovely* and warm.

It is a nice little room.

I've got the use of a cold tap halfway down the stairs and the other thing is just down the bottom of the stairs and across the yard. Yes, it is, very convenient.

Oh, I keep busy. I'm always up to something.

Well, just now it's kettle holders. Someone come in here and asked me to make some for a sale of work or bazaar or fête or that, so I said, well, you get me the materials and I'll make you the kettle holders. I've made dozens.

Would you like one?

I'd like you to have one. Oh, I can spare it. I've got them, here, in a plastic bag. Wonder what we did without plastic. I've got a special one I'd like you to have. It's got a rose on it — where are you? — Here we are.

Isn't it pretty?

No, go on; you have it. I like a little kettle holder. I think it's cheerful. You come into the kitchen and there it is.

Well, it was ever so good of you to come round to tell me about the outing but I don't think I'll bother. Well, the sea's the same wherever you see it, isn't it.

Oh, I'll have a holiday.

I'll take a day off and I won't make a kettle holder!

1969

264

Private 'I'

Music by William Blezard

They say computers are taking over,
They're going to know all
About us all!

No more privacy — no one is excepted
The great, the grand, the humble
And the small,
Have we no defence?
No sovereign rights at all?

We've got the right to be private,
The right to be individual,
The right to be what we are
And what we are is private.

We hold the key to our conscience,
This is a right and we yield to nobody,
No computer controls the mind
For we've got the right to be private.

This is what our right is,
This is what we proclaim:
I'm *not* a number

I'm not a cypher
No, I'm a private 'I' — with a name.
A NAME.

We've got the right,
We've got the right
— to be private.

Each in his own impregnable citadel
Where we're boss, and what's more,
That's the law! and what's more,
We've got the right to be private, private.
'PRIVATE'

First Flight

Like 'Boat Train' this is about selfless mother-love, a perilous subject for the theatre. Goodness is almost impossible to show on the stage. It calls for simplicity that is neither dull nor empty and for humility that is in no way false. Once again I knew that it could work only if treated lightly and with faint self-mockery. The sketch is about a woman in an aeroplane on her way to America to meet her son's black American wife and the grandchildren she has never seen. I couldn't find the right voice for it until I tried it out in an unlocalised North Country accent. Then it fell into place. There is a directness in North Country speech that suggests honesty (though it can also suggest narrowness and that wouldn't do for the country woman I was after). If the speech were too brisk it suggested smugness, so I worked on trying to get a gentleness that was at the same time sure and strong, but never dogmatic or opinionated. I wanted to show her as a woman of natural loving instincts, disturbed by her reaction to the situation, longing to be able to stand by the belief she holds dearly that all men are one in the sight of God, and much concerned

267

that she may not be able to hide the ambi-
valence of feeling she hadn't expected to
have and so longs to be without. 'I do want
to do it right,' she says. 'I just want to do it
right.' I hoped the audience would feel
confident that she did.

Scene: in a transatlantic aeroplane.

Oh, the little light's come on.

'Fasten your seat belt' — well, I will if I can. I've had too much lunch. Can you manage?

I never saw anybody work so hard as you — all the way over, through lunch. I said to myself, 'I bet he's on a business trip.' Yes, I thought you were.

No, I'm on a holiday.

Yes, it is my first visit to America. Of course, you know just what it is going to look like, don't you. Films and television, and that. I think it's a shame really. I'd like to have been surprised. Well, perhaps it will feel different when you're there.

Oh — ooh — what's that? Bumpy.

A cloud? Oh. Yes — look — the window's gone all white. Ah, blue again, that's better. We are coming down, you can see; yes, there it is.

It is my first flight. Well, it's not actually my *first* flight. I flew to the Channel Islands once, but I didn't like it. I came back by boat! Silly. But this is my first proper flight, with food. And I like the souvenir picture-postcard they've given us of the plane. I'm going to give it to my grandchildren; they'll have to draw lots to see who gets it.

Don't you want yours? You sure? I wasn't dropping a hint. Well, I'd love to have it if you can spare it, thank you very much. I'll tell them I sat next to a very nice man on the plane and he gave me his postcard.

I've never seen my grandchildren yet. Well, I haven't seen my son for over five years. He's in electronics. He went out on a contract, and he didn't know if he'd like it, but he did and he's settled. He's had several promotions — they think very highly of him — and when the last one came he wrote and said, 'Come on over, Mum,' and he's given me the trip.

Yes, it is nice. Yes, he is, he's very bright, but he's not spoiled with it. They're going to meet me at the airport in New York. They live near a place called Stamford, Connect-ti-cutt. Oh, is that how you pronounce it! Well, I won't have to mention it when I'm there, and I can learn it for when I go home. Yes, his wife is American.

She's an Afro-American — a coloured girl.

I do hope I'll do it all right.

When the letter came I . . . I didn't really know what I thought, but I've brought up Kev — that's my son — and his sister, to believe that it isn't *who* you are — it's what you are that matters. And I really do believe that.

I suppose it's an awful thing to say, but you know in some ways I'm glad his dad . . . I lost him six years ago and he was a dear man, but he didn't like change. He liked everything to go just like it always had done. Pattern. He liked what he knew . . . I think he might have found the adjustment . . . a bit . . .

But my father! Oh my father! He loved changes if they were a good idea. And he loved people. He could always get right to the middle of a person — anybody. He was outspoken but not just for hearing his own voice. He was very well liked. He was a gardener; and he said you have lots of time to think; you put something in the ground and you have to wait for it to come up. He was a lovely man. I thought the world

269

of my father.

I could do with having him with me here now, I can tell you . . .

I don't know whether I think it's easier for a mixed marriage in England or America. I think there's more of them in America. But I wish they were living near me, you know, with the children running in and out of the house.

But I don't know. People are very narrow where I live. They have such *little* lives. None of them use their front rooms. They've all got them and they keep them lovely but they don't live in them. Matching nets on all the windows . . . but they don't use their front rooms.

D'you know there's a woman in my Church said to me 'I don't know why you go on about us all being the same. I mean, I look in the mirror and I'm pink, and they look in the mirror and they're brown. We *are* different; we're meant to be different.'

I thought to meself 'Well, I'm glad I'm different from you.' Well, she's got some very funny false teeth. I shouldn't have said that. It wasn't kind. But she gets on my wick.

I said to her: 'Look, people are always going to look different to people, but in the sight of God we are all absolutely the same — I'm sure of it.' I hope you didn't mind me saying that? Well, people don't like you to mention God. They get all embarrassed and start counting their buttons. But I'm used to it. My father talked a lot about God.

Oh, look — we really are coming down. All those little cars — pastel coloured — pink and blue. And the back gardens — there's one with a swimming-pool and laundry. Can you see? Oh, you've seen it before.

Oh — they've those brakes on much too fast. The

270

whole place is shuddering. I don't like it. Are you sure it's all right? Oh there's the music come on. I'm glad to hear it. You must think me silly — oh dear . . .

Yes. There are two grandchildren, a girl and a boy. I've got lovely snaps of them — one is very, very dark, but the other . . . honestly . . . you'd never know . . . I've got lovely snaps of her, too. She's beautiful. Very tall and slim, and, of course, Kev would never marry someone who wasn't nice.

They met at a concert. He's very musical, is Kev. Opera mostly, and he has a marvellous collection of gramophone records, but of course he didn't take them with him when he went to America because he didn't know if he would settle, but he did and he sent for them. Have you ever had to send anyone a *lot* of gramophone records? Well — don't! It's awful!

She writes me such lovely letters. She calls me Mother Comstock. 'Dear Mother Comstock' — I'm Mrs Comstock you see. I think it's nice. It's got a sort of bouncy rhythm — Mother Comstock.

When I think of my mother-in-law . . . I never called her anything for twenty-five years! Except 'dear' in a time of crisis. Now and then I'd say Mrs C. and she liked it. I should have done it more often.

Do you think there is a place where they could watch for the plane coming? Observation Terraces, don't they call them, or something? They have one at London Airport I think . . .

Well, we are swinging round. There is a building coming into view with people on the roof terrace . . .

They're there.

They're all there . . .

Oh, I do *hope* I do it all right.

I just want to do it right.

1969

Mulgarth Street

Yes — it is a beautiful flat —
We come here from Mulgarth Street,
D'you know it?
It was hell on earth.
We lived there for thirty years or more,
Terrible dump, old Mulgarth Street,
Most terrible dump you ever saw.
Wallpaper peeling off, dark and damp
And there was rats.
And that awful smell — you know —
And gas *and* cats.
But I'd rather be there now, I swear I would,
Than stuck up here
In these high, horrible, beautiful modern flats.

Nobody never pops in and says,
'How are you today, dear,
Can you lend us a dab of marge,
Pay you back on pay day.'
Stuck up here on the sixteenth floor
Nobody never goes past the door,
You can't hear the ice-cream music now,
I haven't seen the dustman for months,
We shouldn't of come here, that's for sure.

Life down there in Mulgarth Street was rich all
    right!
We all knew what went on and where.
Up here? Looking out the window
Makes you feel so queer
And you can't see what goes on from here.
Look like a lot of ants down there.
People keep their selves to themselves in flats.
This is a toffee-nosed address.
Nobody knows if you're dead or alive,
And nobody couldn't care less.

Oh yes, Mulgarth Street was hell on earth
It was a scandal — and a disgrace.
Talk about slums! — You couldn't have found a
    worser place.

But it was friendly.
Neighbourly and that.
People had time for a cupper and a chat.
It was civilised.
Not like up here — stuck up here
In this high, horrible, beautiful modern flat.

They've torn it down, old Mulgarth Street,
I went along and saw.
Bulldozed it down — old Mulgarth Street.
None of it's not there no more.
Tst. Tst.
I don't know.
But where's it gone to, all that friendliness
And that fun?
It must be somewhere.

1971

In the Green Time of
Moon Daisies

Music by Joyce Grenfell

In the green time of moon daisies wild roses wild
  roses moon daisies and buttercups,
In the green, green, green time of summer I
  remember being young.

Wide green fields, high wide skies,
The lark's song rising clear,
Honeybees in the scented flowers,
Zooming near.

In the green time of cow parsley elderberry
  elderberry cow parsley and buttercups.
In the green, green, white green time of summer I
  remember songs we sung.

In the green time of clover honeysuckle
  honeysuckle white clover and buttercups
In the green, green, green time of summer I
  remember being young —
I remember how it felt to be young.
(Oh, the joy of it, oh, the *hell* of it — being
  young!)

III
NURSERY SCHOOL
SKETCHES

Going Home Time

It is winter

Children — it's time to go home, so finish tidying up and put on your hats and coats. Some of our Mummies are here for us, so hurry up.

Billy won't be long, Mrs Binton. He's on hamster duty.

Now let's see if we can't all help each other.

Janey — I said help each other. Help Bobbie carry that chair, don't pin him against the wall with it.

We're having a go at our good neighbour policy here, Mrs Binton, but it doesn't always . . .

Neville, off the floor, please. Don't lie there.

And Sidney, stop painting, please.

Because it's time to go home.

Well, you shouldn't have started another picture, should you. What is it this time?

Another blue man! Oh, I see, so it is.

All right, you can make it just a little bit bluer, but only one more brushful, please, Sidney.

We don't think he's very talented, but we feel it's important to encourage their self-expression. You never know where it might lead . . .

Rachel. Gently — help Teddy *gently* into his coat.

It's a lovely coat, Teddy, what's wrong with it?

Oh. It looks like a boy's coat when you wear it. And lots of boys wear pink.

Poor wee mite, he has three older sisters!

Neville, I said get up off the floor.

Who shot you dead?

David did? Well, I don't suppose he meant to. He may have meant to then, but he doesn't mean it now, and anyhow I say you can get up.

No, don't go and shoot David dead, because it's time to go home.

George. What did I tell you not to do? Well, don't do it.

And Sidney, don't wave that paint-brush about like that, you'll splash somebody. LOOK OUT, DOLORES!

Sidney! . . . It's all right, Dolores, you aren't hurt, you're just surprised. It was only a nice soft brush. But you'd better go and wash your face before you go home.

Because it's all blue.

Sidney, I saw you deliberately put that paintbrush up Dolores's little nostril.

No, it wasn't a jolly good shot. It was . . . I don't want to discuss it, Sidney.

Now go and tell Dolores you're sorry.

Yes, now.

Thank you, Hazel, for putting the chairs straight for me.

You are a great helper.

Thank you.

And thank you, Dicky, for closing the cupboard door for me.

Dicky, is there somebody *in* the cupboard?

Well, let her out at once.

Are you all right, Peggy? What did you go into the cupboard for?

But we don't have mices — I mean mouses — in our

toy cupboard. Mouses only go where there is food, and we don't have any food in our toy cupboard.

When did you hide a bicky in there?

Every day!

Well, perhaps we have got mices in our toy cupboard. I'll have to look.

No, you go and get your coat on.

Dicky — We never shut people in cupboards.

Because they don't like it.

What do you mean, she's puggy? Peggy's puggy?

Oh, she's got puggy hands. But you don't have to hold her hand . . .

Well, you must ask her nicely to let go.

Well, if she won't let go . . .

You'll have to work it out for yourself, Dicky.

Edgar and Timmy — your knitted caps are not for playing tug-of-war with. Look, now the pom-pom's come off.

Whose is it?

Well, give it back to Sidney.

Where are your caps?

Well, go and ask Sidney to give them back to you.

Turn round, Geoffrey. You've got your wellingtons on the wrong feet.

Yes, you have. You'll have to take them off and start again.

Why can't you reach?

Well, undo your coat and then you can bend.

Take off your woolly gloves.

And your scarf.

You can keep your balaclava on. How many jerseys are you wearing?

Heavens. No wonder you can't bend.

Caroline, come and help Geoffrey.

Don't kick her, Geoffrey. She's come to help.

279

Sidney, I told you to put that paint-brush down …
LOOK OUT, DOLORES!

Well, *that* wasn't a very good shot, was it? You didn't mean to put it in her ear, did you?

Well, you shouldn't have.

You're all right Dolores. It was just a bit of a surprise, but you'll have to go and wash again.

Because you've got a blue ear.

Sidney, I'm ashamed of you, a big boy of four, and she's only just three.

And Sidney, what have you done with Timmy and Edgar's caps?

No, I'm not going to guess.

And I don't want to know they are hidden in a special secret place, I want to know exactly where they are.

No, I'm not going to try and find them. You're going to tell me where they are.

Well, go and get them out of the waste-paper basket at once. Waste-paper baskets aren't for putting caps in.

Now go and say you are sorry to Dolores.

Yes, again.

We think his aggression is diminishing, but we do have setbacks.

Lavinia, is that your coat you've got on? It looks so enormous.

Oh, you're going to grow into it. I see.

Hazel, thank you for helping Betty into her jacket.

Just zip her up once. Not up and down.

No, Neville, you can't have a turn.

No, children, you can't all zip Betty.

Jenny, come here.

Jenny, when we have paid a visit to the littlest room, what do we do?

We pull our knickers up again.

280

Good-bye, Hazel, Good-bye, Bobbie. Good-bye, everybody.

Good-bye, Mrs Binton.

Hurry up, Sidney, because you'll keep your Mummy waiting.

Well, your Granny then.

Somebody is coming to take you away, aren't they, Sidney?

Good.

No, you won't see me tomorrow, Sidney.

Tomorrow is Saturday, thank heaven.

Free Activity Period

Oh, hello, Mrs Hingle. I'm so glad you could come along. As you see, we're just having a Free Activity Period, and in our Free Activity Period each little individual chooses his or her own occupation. Some are painting, some are using plasticine, and some work at a sand-table. We feel that each little one must get to the bottom of his or her self and find out what he really wants of life.

Who is making that buzzing noise?

Well, stop it please, Neville.

Hazel, dear, come away from the door and get on with your plasticine.

I love to see them so happily occupied, each one expressing his little personality . . .

George – don't do that . . .

Now, children, I want you all to say 'Good morning' to Mrs Hingle. Good morning, Mrs Hingle.

No, Sidney, not good-bye. Mrs Hingle has only just come. You don't want her to go away yet?

No, she hasn't got a funny hat on, that's her hair.

So sorry, Mrs Hingle. Sometimes we ARE just a trifle outspoken. We try to encourage honesty, only sometimes it doesn't always . . .

And this is my friend Caroline, and Caroline is paint-ing such a lovely red picture, aren't you, Caroline? I wonder what it is? Perhaps it's a lovely red sunset, is it? Or a big red orange?

It's a picture of Mummy! For a moment I thought it was a big red orange, but now you tell me, I can see it is a picture of Mummy.

Aren't you going to give her any nose?

No nose.

It's so interesting the way they see things.

Sidney, don't blow at Edgar, please.

I know I said you could choose what you are going to do, but you cannot choose to blow at Edgar.

Because it isn't a good idea.

Yes, I know it makes his hair go up and down, but I don't want you to do it. Now get back to the sand-table, there's a good boy.

Yes, there is room, Sue; there's heaps of room. Just move up a bit.

Susan! We *never* bite our friends.

Say you are sorry to Sidney. You needn't kiss him. No, you needn't hug him. Susan, PUT HIM DOWN. No fisticuffs, please.

She hasn't made any teeth marks, has she, Sidney? Well then . . . don't fuss.

Sometimes our little egos are on the big side, I'm afraid . . .

Hazel, dear, I don't want to have to say it again: please come away from the door.

Why can't you?

Well, you shouldn't have put your finger in the key-hole, and then it wouldn't have got stuck.

Children, there is no need for everyone to come and have a look just because poor Hazel has caught her finger in the keyhole. Back to your work, please.

No, Sidney, I don't think it is stuck in there for ever and ever.

I don't for one minute think we will have to get the Fire Brigade to come and take the door down to set her free. You do exaggerate, Sidney.

Well, if we haven't got her finger out by dinner-time she'll have to have it here.

And her tea.

And her supper and stay the night.

But we are going to get it out, aren't we, Hazel?

David. Turn round, please, David. Right round.

Use your hanky, please, David.

And again.

And again.

And now wipe.

Thank you, David.

Hazel, why did you put your finger in the keyhole?

To see if it would go in!

Well, now let's see if we can get it out!

Who is making that buzzing noise?

Neville.

I know you are a busy bee, but boy busy-bees don't buzz. Only bee busy-bees buzz.

I can still hear you, Neville.

Neville!

I should think so.

He's such a musical child, and one doesn't want to discourage him.

Sidney, take that paint-brush out of your ear and give it back to Lavinia.

Yes, you do want it back, Lavinia. You like painting. Yes, you do.

We're hoping she is going to take to it soon.

Now then, Hazel, have you tried wiggling it?

You know, Mrs Hingle, this child's finger really is caught in the keyhole . . . I think the Fire Brigade are the best in an emergency. Yes, there is a telephone —

at the end of the passage. Would you? Oh, that is good of you. I'll stay here and hold the fort and prepare the children. Thank you so much.

Children, I don't want anyone to get excited, but kind Mrs Hingle has gone to see if we can get one of those clever men from the Fire Brigade to come and help us get Hazel's finger out . . .

Oh, you've got it out, Hazel. Well done. That's lovely.
IT'S ALL RIGHT, MRS HINGLE — SHE'S GOT IT OUT.

Sidney. You are not to go near the keyhole.
SIDNEY.

Can you get it out?
I SPOKE TOO SOON, MRS HINGLE . . .
Oh, Sidney . . .

Nativity Play

Hello, Mrs Binton. I'm so glad you could get along to see a rehearsal of our Nativity Play! Can you squeeze in there? I'm afraid our chairs are a wee bitty wee, as they say north of the border!

Now then, children. We are going to start our rehearsal. Where are my Mary and Joseph?

That's right, Shirleen, take Denis by the hand and come and sit nice and quietly on this bench in the middle.

Don't drag him. He'll come if you leave him alone!

Don't hit each other, Mary and Joseph were *friends*.

Now, who are my Wise Men?

You're a Wise Man, aren't you, Geoffrey?

Oh, aren't you? What are you then?

Oh, you're a cattle, are you? And you are going to low. Splendid! Go over to Miss Boulting, will you, please?

Miss Boulting . . . You are organising the animals and the angels? He is one of yours.

Now, my Wise Men here, please!

Billy, Peter and George.

And George, Wise Men never do that . . .

Now my Kings, please.

Of course, Mrs Binton, we know that by tradition the Wise Men and the Kings are one and the same, but

286

we did want everyone in our Nursery School Nativity Play to have a chance, so we have taken a few liberties, and I don't think any one will mind.

Now Kings: Sidney, Neville, Cliff and Nikolas Anoniodes.

Four Kings, I'm afraid. We happen to have four lovely crowns, so it seemed a pity not to use them.

Sidney, put your crown on *straight* please, not over one eye. What have you got under your jersey?

That's not the place for a hamster, is it. Put him straight back in his little pen, please.

Sidney, which one have you got, Paddington or Harold Wilson?

Well, who's got Paddington?

Neville, put him back at once.

Poor Paddington and Harold Wilson, it isn't very Christmassy for them under your jersey.

Sidney, I think it serves your right if Harold Wilson bit you, and don't bite him back.

Because he's smaller than you are. Are you bleeding?

Then don't make such a fuss.

Cliff, put your crown on, please.

It's too big? Let's see. Ah, yes it is . . .

Where are you! Oh, there you are! Nice to see you again! Change with Nikolas.

Nikolas, you can manage a big crown, can't you? You've got just the ears for it.

I think if you pull your ears down a bit that will hold it up. And lean back a bit. That's it.

Stay like that, dear. Don't move.

Wise Men and Kings, don't muddle yourselves with each other.

Now then, Shepherds.

Jimmy, you are my First Shepherd and not a racing car.

Yes, Caroline, you're a shepherd.

No, dear you can't wear your Little Bo-Peep costume: because there aren't any little girl shepherdesses in our play. They're all boy shepherds, and you are a girl being a boy shepherd.

Yes, it is rotten. But we just have to settle for it. I think if you are very good perhaps you can wear a lovely grey beard; wouldn't that be fun?

George, what do Wise Men never do?

Yes . . .

Jimmy, do you remember what you see up in the sky? Something lovely, isn't it?

No, not a baby. Try again.

It's a lovely silver star, and you are going to put your hand up and point to it. And what are you going to say when you do that?

No, Sidney, he isn't going to say, 'Please may I go to the bathroom?'

Children, that isn't funny; it's a perfectly natural function, and we might as well get used to it.

Come on, Jimmy. You are going to say, 'Behold!' aren't you?

Yes, you are, dear. You said it yesterday.

You'd rather say it tomorrow?

Perhaps you are right.

We have broken the back of the play, so you may as well get ready to go home. Hand in your crowns gently, please. No Sidney, you can't wear your crown home on the bus.

I think — I HOPE it will be all right on the night.

But you know, Mrs Binton, I think perhaps next year we might make do with a Christmas carol.